A REIMAGINING
OF RELATI

CW01654193

JADE MONTSERRAT

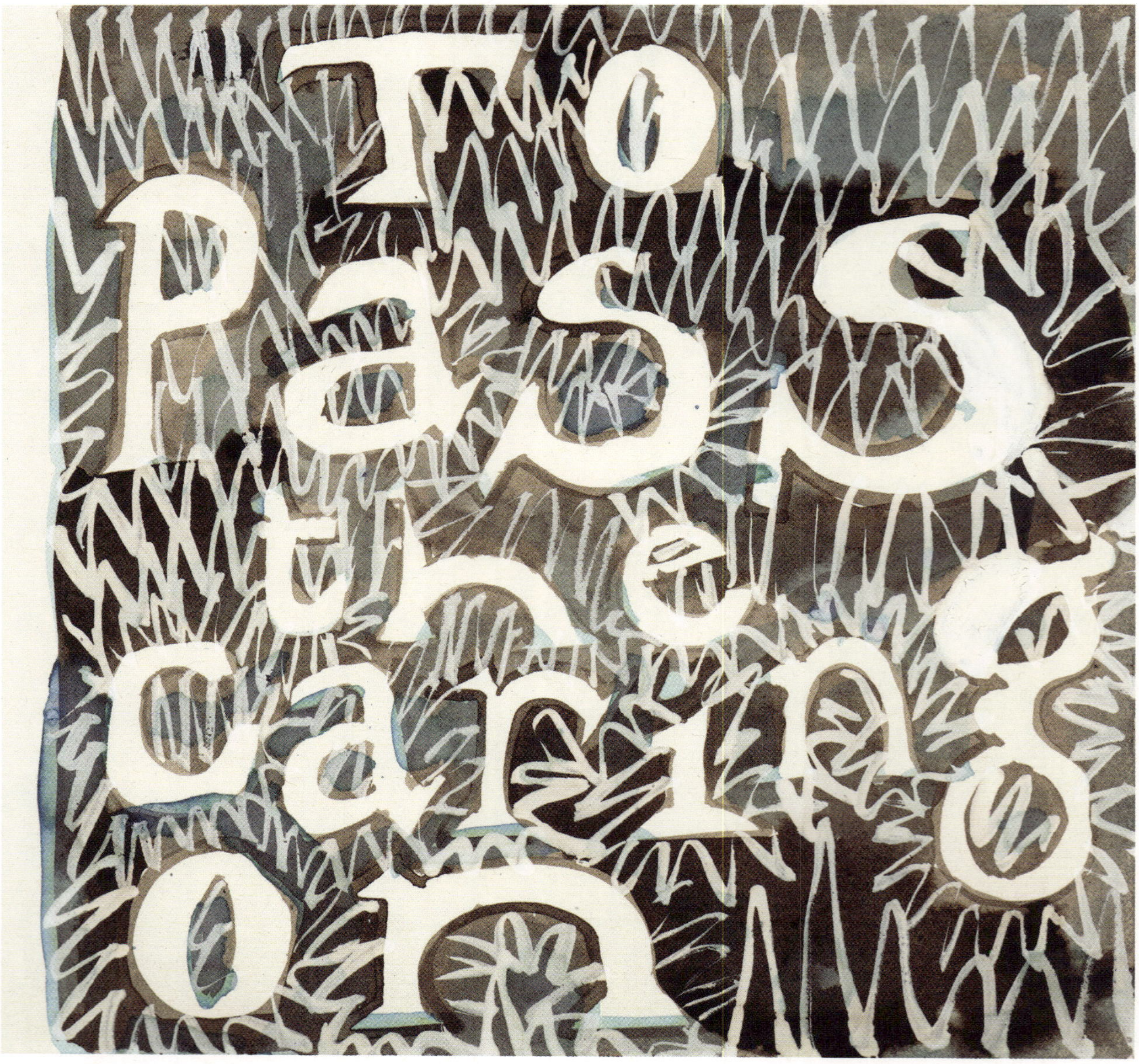

To pass the caring on, 2021

DEDICATED TO

IRA ALDRIDGE,
FREEDOM FIGHTERS
AND ABOLITIONISTS
WORLDWIDE.

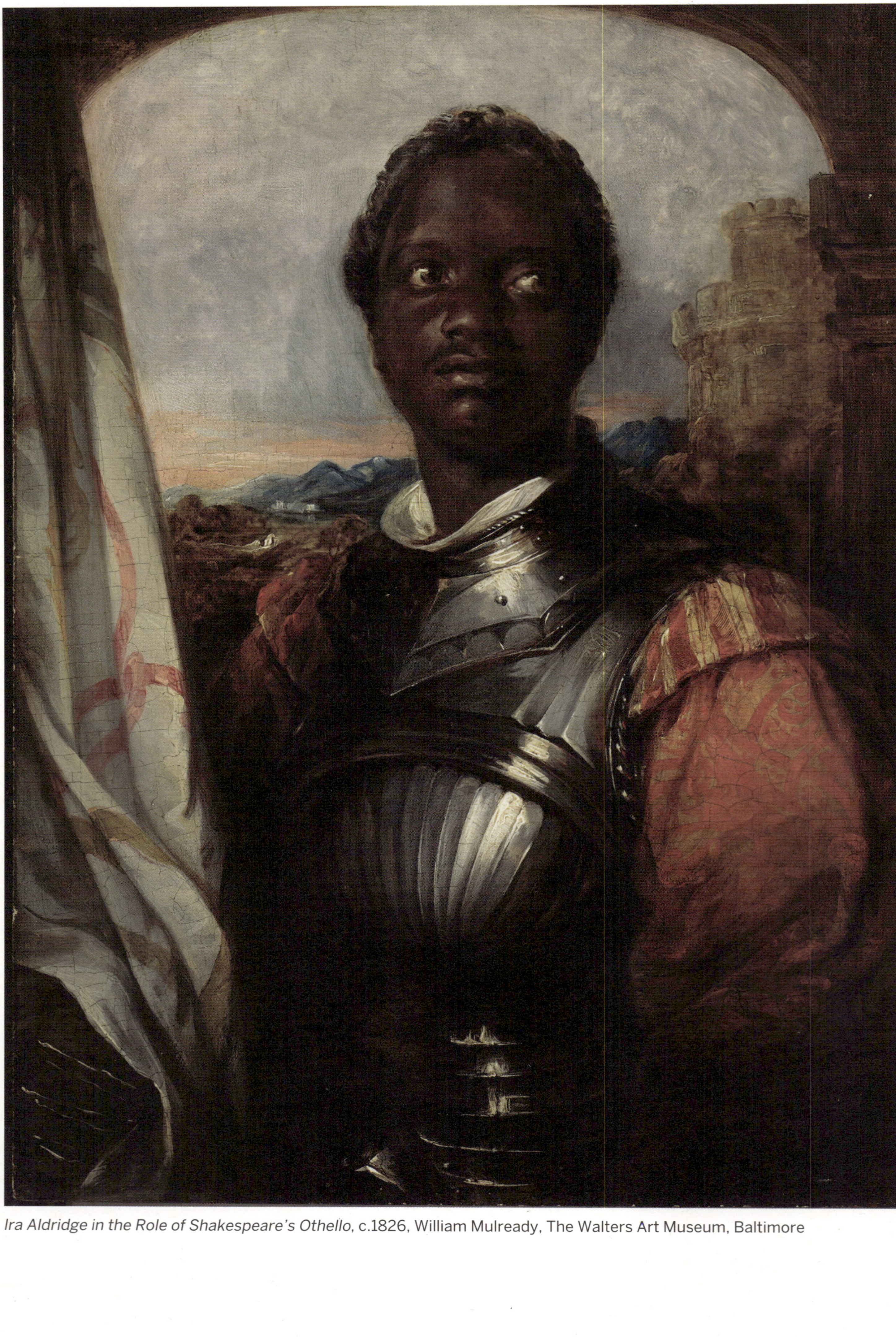

Ira Aldridge in the Role of Shakespeare's Othello, c.1826, William Mulready, The Walters Art Museum, Baltimore

ORDER OF PLAY

07 FOREWORD

11 ACT I: IRA — CURIOSITY AND CREATIVE LANGUAGE

23 IN CONVERSATION: KATE JESSON AND SANDY NAIRNE

31 ACT II: SCORING PERFORMANCE

41 BLACK PANTHER PARTY: THE TEN-POINT PROGRAM

47 IN CONVERSATION: NIKITA GILL AND JADE MONTSERRAT

67 ACT III: ON PUBLISHING RADICAL CONSTITUTIONS

81 INVISIBILITY, FUGITIVITY AND HYPERVISIBILITY: EXPLORING BLACK ATLANTIC LIVES IN THE NORTH OF ENGLAND WITH JADE MONTSERRAT BY ALAN RICE

90 LIST OF WORKS
91 ACKNOWLEDGEMENTS
95 CONTRIBUTORS
99 IMAGE CREDITS

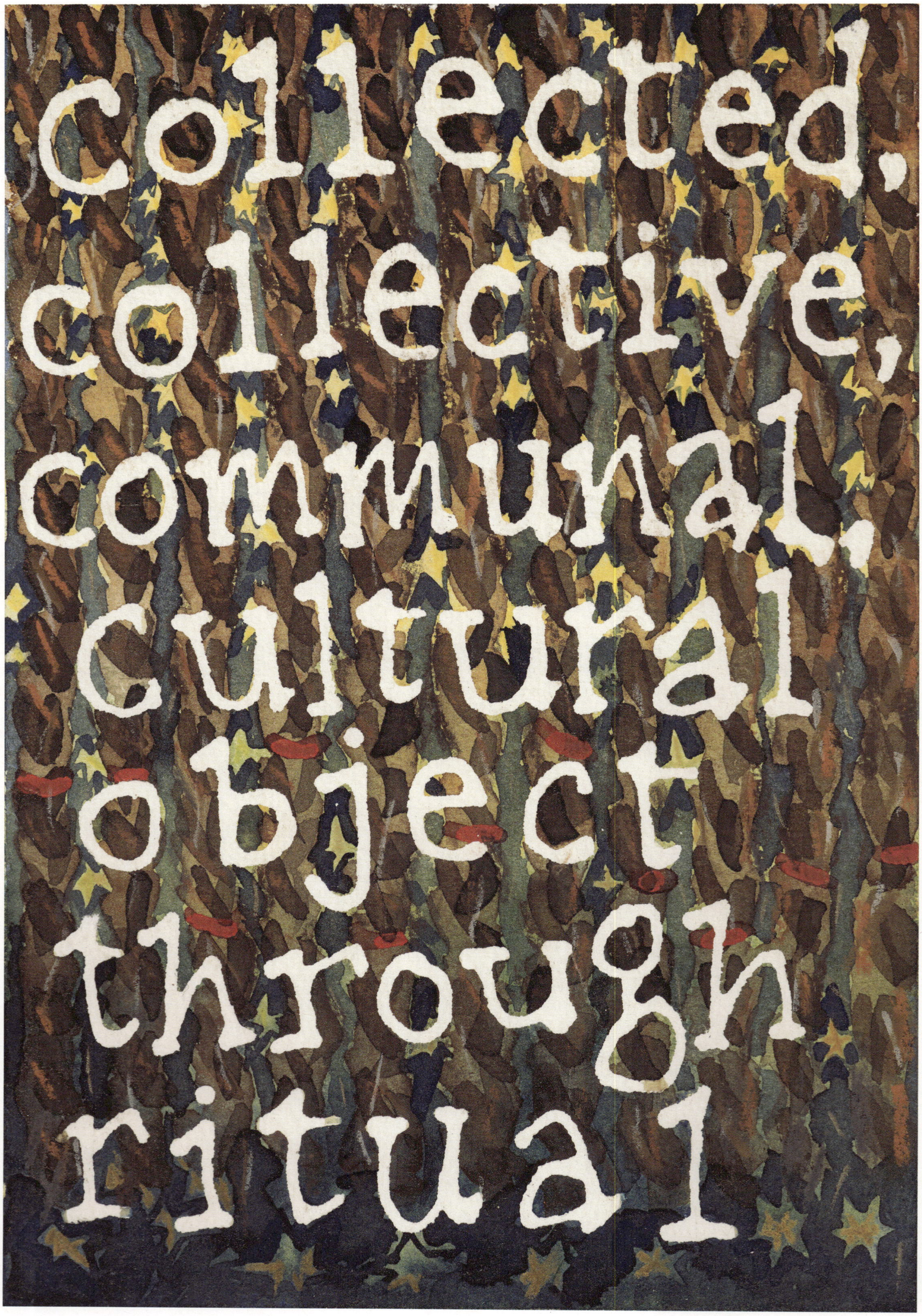

Collected, collective, communal, cultural object through ritual, 2021

FOREWORD

In the national conference *Whose Heritage? The Impact of Cultural Diversity on Britain's Living Heritage* held in Manchester in November 1999, the sociologist, cultural theorist and political activist Stuart Hall made a call to action for a reimagined Britain for all who refuse to become othered in order to belong. This call to action remains just as relevant and urgent for our national collections within visual arts museums and galleries today.

Jade Montserrat's artist publication, *A Reimagining of Relations*, speaks to the heart of this call, asking us not only to consider but also to enact new models needed for commissioning and collecting art. Jade's commission is the first in *Future Collect*, an ambitious three-year partnership project initiated by iniva (Institute of International Visual Art), which reimagines the future of collecting within major visual arts institutions. *Future Collect* commemorates iniva's 25th anniversary in 2019 and aspires to create a legacy far beyond it. iniva works to bring about change that reflects the ongoing expansion of contemporary art practices, as well as the histories and transformations of identities across British culture and society.

For this inaugural commission in the *Future Collect* series iniva, in partnership with Manchester Art Gallery, invited artist Jade Montserrat supported by curator Nikita Gill, to contribute a thoughtful and critical work to Manchester's collection. The artist's proposal and collaboration with the staff at iniva and Manchester Art Gallery goes far beyond our anticipated outcomes of addressing questions around the intersection of culture, class and politics found within the existing collection. Jade's practice pushes further, compelling us to think about what it means to build an infrastructure of care for artists, artworks, and their narratives for gallery audiences.

Over the course of two years, Jade's generous artistic response to the commission has included conversations with her peers staged in three acts; *Act I: Ira — Curiosity and Creative Language, Act II: Scoring Performance* and *Act III: On Publishing Radical Constitutions.* In November 2020 Jade's exhibition, entitled *Constellations: Care & Resistance*, included works from the Manchester Art Gallery collection by Claudette Johnson, Ian Hamilton Finlay and Mark Titchner alongside Jade's happening *Drawing Out* performed with Nikita Gill. Together with the commission the artist has shaped and guided a series of study days and a conference, to further expand and deepen our understanding of the context for her work and those from the collection. Her exhibition with the final commissioned work for Manchester Art Gallery's collection includes the performance *Rehearsal Methods: audition pieces for solo and collective*, 2021, a set of props, a series of drawings and this publication. The exhibition will be accompanied by a community and learning programme to widen the participation and reach of this project.

A Reimagining of Relations speaks to Jade's transdisciplinary approach as an artist, through the careful, considered collaboration and thinking that forms this strong body of work. The project was initiated by her curiosity in the very first painting collected by the Royal Manchester Institution for the Promotion of Literature, Science and the Arts in 1827 (this collection is now part of the Manchester Art Gallery collection). A distinct and notable purchase of a James

Northcote portrait of actor Ira Aldridge posing in character as William Shakespeare's Othello, in the dramatic scene in Act III where Othello hears of his wife Desdemona's apparent betrayal. The painting has featured in many rehangs of the Gallery's collection. Jade's commission asks us to consider the story that lies behind the man in the painting: who he was, and what his story tells us about changing attitudes in British society.

This provocation comes at a key moment in the history of Manchester Art Gallery, which is approaching its 200th anniversary at a time when the coronavirus pandemic has lifted a veil on deep social inequalities and accelerated the need to rethink how cultural institutions work in a globalised environment. This project has been central to recalibrating the Gallery's priorities during more than a year of national lockdowns, representing the first time it has been forced to close in its entire history. Working closely but remotely with Jade during this period has permeated the institution with the mindset and indomitable spirit of the artist in ways that would not have otherwise transpired, and in some ways given this process more urgency and intensity.

The *Future Collect* collaboration has occupied the forefront of our minds as Manchester Art Gallery prepares for the next 200 years, completely rethinking the purpose and intended audience of the collection. Throughout its life the Gallery has been driven by the social imperative of holding a collection intended to play an active part in the lives of the city's residents, owned by every resident of the city by its constitution. As such, it is not required that the Gallery continues collecting for the sake of building ever-larger-holdings. Rather it must work with artists and partners such as iniva to rebalance and retune the collections of the city, that they may remain relevant and useful for the public.

Caring for people, as well as objects, is a fundamental concern for iniva and Manchester Art Gallery. This is not easily achieved with a collection formed in other eras and other contexts, in which the meanings of the objects were constructed from a predominately monocultural standpoint. We have to acknowledge that Manchester Art Gallery is fully entangled in the history of industry, commerce, patriarchy and empire. However, the roots of the city are also entwined in histories of rebellion, dissent and the pursuit of justice and equality. Working with artists, curators and a wide network of collaborators has teased out new threads, shown new ways forward, demodernising and decolonising in a way that enriches the way we advance knowledge, and re-opens the capacity of art for all society.

iniva and Manchester Art Gallery wish to thank all the artists, individuals, funders and organisations who have helped to make this exhibition, commission and publication happen:

Firstly Jade, who made a bold and audacious step in being the first artist commissioned for *Future Collect*. We have learnt so much from working with her and witnessing her unwavering resolve to place care at the centre of her work. This project has been supported by the *Future Collect* team, we are thankful for the ground work and initiation of the project by iniva former director Melanie Keen and the commitment to securing the funding from iniva Development Manager

Jenny Starr. We have been fortunate to work with a dedicated group from iniva and Manchester Art Gallery: Curatorial Project Manager Rohini Malik Okon whose calm temperance has seen the project through to completion; Curator-in-training Nikita Gill, whose creative contributions and research have built a critical yet caring framework for Jade's work; Curator Kate Jesson, who has been a guiding mentor and knowledgeable asset in the development of this project. As the project has gathered momentum the *Future Collect* project team were also joined joined by Dr. Alison Rooke drawing out insightful reflections to evaluate the project, Anahí Saravia-Herrera as Programme Producer and Priya Jay leading on the curatorial network *Future Commons*, whose contributions have been thoughtful, responsive and far-reaching beyond our expectations. This book is eloquently designed by Rose Nordin as the first artist publication for the publishing platform STUART. We are thankful for the creative editors Industria who have worked closely with Jade on this publication with support from our copy-editor Jay Drinkall.

Whilst this publication is one part of the commission, we are grateful to the excellent support that iniva and Manchester Art Gallery have provided over the course of the last two years. Our gratitude to iniva board of trustees chaired by Anita Bhalla and to the team; Adrian Harper, Tavian Hunter, Sarah Mangan, Sae Matsuno, Simina Neagu, Susan Skingle, Jenny Starr, and Stefania Valente at iniva. At Manchester Art Gallery with thanks to Dave Carden, Emma Carroll and the Art of Resilience team, Russ Clark, Shamus Dawes, Martin Grimes, Claire Grundy, Bev Hogg, Natasha Howes, Megan Lang, Charles McKenzie, Phillippa Milner, Catriona Morgan, Mark Page, Meg Parnell, the Visitor Services team, John Ward and the volunteer guides and Hannah Williamson.

We are indebted to the ongoing support of Arts Council England, Art Fund and the Esmée Fairbairn Foundation, without which this project would not have been possible. They have all shown great understanding and reassurance through the coronavirus pandemic, and their ongoing commitment and belief in the project has held us in good stead to continue with *Future Collect.*

Sepake Angiama, Artistic Director, iniva

Alistair Hudson, Director of the Whitworth and Manchester Art Gallery

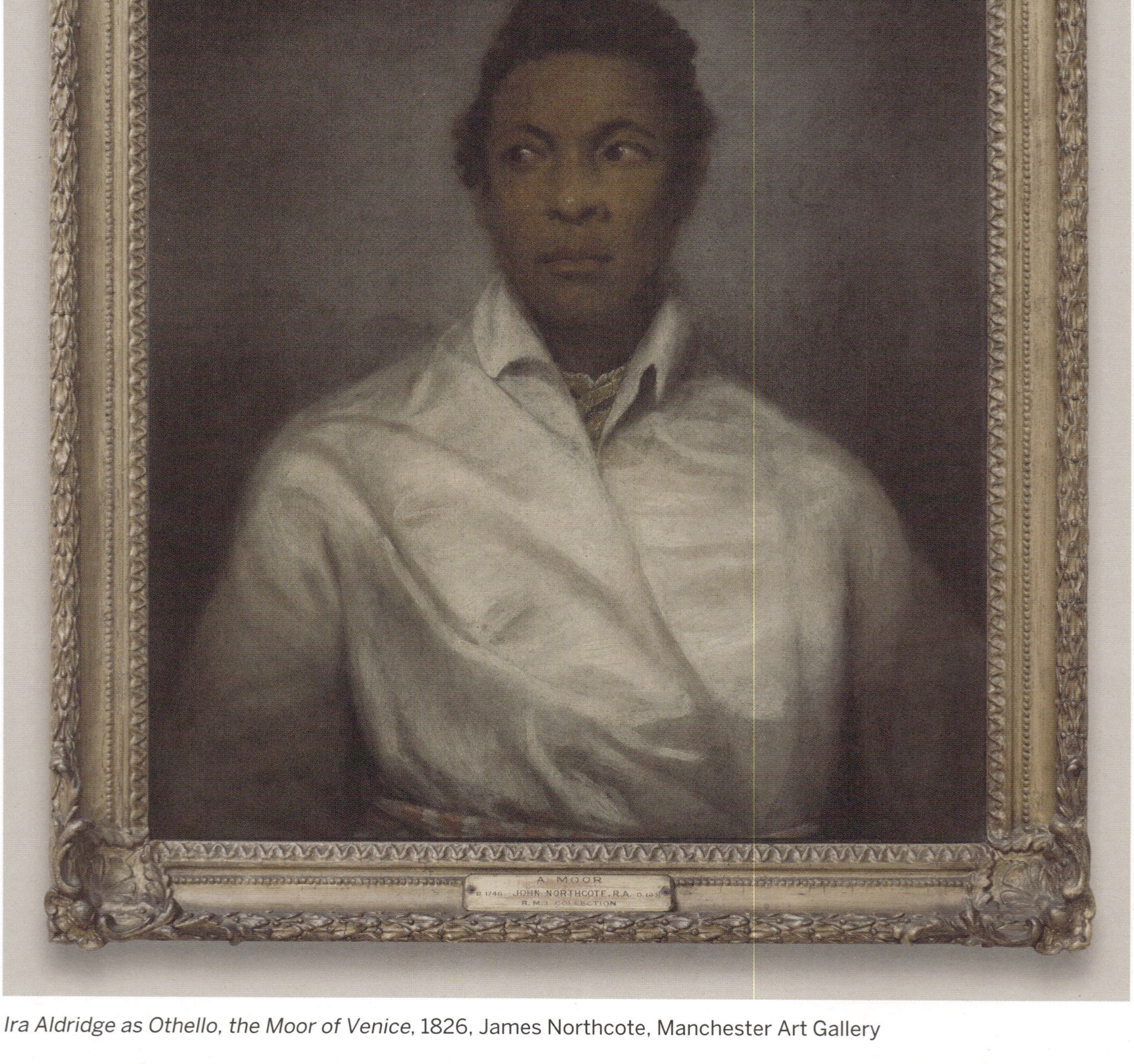

Ira Aldridge as Othello, the Moor of Venice, 1826, James Northcote, Manchester Art Gallery

Previously titled *Head of a Negro in the Character of Othello* (1826), *Othello, the Moor of Venice* (1827), *A Moor* (1846). Title changed to *Ira Aldridge as Othello, the Moor of Venice* in 2020.

ACT I

IRA – CURIOSITY AND CREATIVE LANGUAGE

Ira — Curiosity and Creative Language took place as an online conversation on 28 May 2020. Jade Montserrat was joined by Amber Akaunu and Fauziya Johnson of *ROOT-ed* zine; Maurice Carlin and Rivca Rubin, two of four artistic directors at Islington Mill arts space in Salford; and Kate Jesson, curator at Manchester Art Gallery. The discussion, moderated by Nikita Gill and Chloe Austin, centred around questions of access to art-historical information, and asks how the contextualisation of James Northcote's 1826 painting of Black actor Ira Aldridge provokes urgency in developing new creative languages.

Positing Ira Aldridge as a symbol of resistance, the conversation was shaped by refining and expanding on art institutions' care of collections and care of artists: how societal and historical factors determine care of objects and people, and how creative languages encourage care in the use and ownership of words. In this excerpt from the conversation, the participants explore institutional barriers to curiosity and creativity, possibilities for apology and accountability, and the role of language in addressing and transforming them. Throughout the conversation, the contemporary experience of the speakers is mapped onto Aldridge's own history.

NIKITA GILL

If you don't make things visible, how can you unlock curiosity?

JADE MONTSERRAT

I'm wondering, unless you are introduced to something and have access to it in your formative years, how would you know that it exists at all? I'm thinking about that in relation to belonging to an institution, or trusting an institution. The idea of mirroring, seeing yourself, being heard, being seen, being understood, relates directly to the histories and the stories that we tell. It relates to creative languages, including how we interpret them, and how we listen. Recently I've been relearning how to breathe properly, so that I can feel it in my tummy, and that grounds me. But it took me being able to access yoga to get there. I think there's a similar issue here around visibility and access, and this also links in with hierarchy. If one has had the privilege of seeing themselves, hearing themselves, and really feeling they belong to the historical narrative perpetuated within the society one lives in, then maybe one's curiosity might be stifled because you accept everything. But that belonging might also allow for a certain amount of freedom, because unless you're able to meet your basic needs, it's not possible to prioritise creativity. So I think the answer to the question is that you can't unlock curiosity unless you make things visible — this includes how we communicate, how we care for one another, the silent gestures, and the objects contained in public spaces. It comes back to ownership and access.

FAUZIYA JOHNSON

I agree that this has so much to do with how you grow up. For example, while I was at primary school and high school I never went to an art gallery. My favourite lesson of the week was art and design, but it was only when I went to college and university that my curiosity in art, and everything to do with art, peaked. Since graduating in 2018, the only thing that has kept me curious and interested in the art scene in general is other people talking about what's happening within it and raising issues that need to be raised. In terms of accessibility, nothing deters me from a gallery more than pretentiousness. As a little anecdote, I went to Saatchi Gallery in Chelsea, London, a couple of years back and there was a group of people in front of me who were let into the gallery straight away with their bags. We had bags too but we were told we had to put them in the locker, which I thought just didn't make sense. The only difference between these two groups of people is that we were people of colour and they weren't. From that moment on, I didn't want to be in that gallery. I didn't want to know what was inside, but I thought, 'I'm here now,' because I'd travelled to London from Liverpool with my uni friends.

RIVCA RUBIN

I've noticed that, often, people become curious when there's real curiosity extended to them. By 'real curiosity' I mean that when I'm honestly interested in finding out more about someone, then that tends to be reciprocated. I think that means, rather than me giving you information, or a history that you haven't asked for, instead starting a conversation with: 'What would you like to know about this place, about your visit, about this piece of art?' So there's already an engagement, the person is in control of what they want to know. It would be great if we could stop thinking about communication as a 'skill' that comes out of the toolbox in a professional environment, and that we go home and forget about. I don't think communication is a skill, I think it is an honest interest that comes from a belief in there being a collective 'we' as well as an individual 'you' and 'me' — we've had a very long period of being very 'me, me, me'. I think it's really important to have very uncomfortable conversations, and a lot of them, in a respectful way. I have not met anybody yet who feels particularly motivated to stay in the conversation when they feel they're being accused. However, there is an opportunity to go, 'Okay, that doesn't land well with me, but can you say more?' rather than going on the defensive. It would be great if we could be really, honestly curious about what we have to offer, or show, or share with one another at that moment, whatever that may be.

AMBER AKAUNU

I feel like in conversations around cultural institutions, 'Black people' are often spoken about as if they're separate from the 'general public' and I feel like we have to approach that differently. We have to go back to basics, because institutions are built on racism. For example, Tate Liverpool is on the docks, so the slave trade is in the history of that building, but they don't do things for Black History Month and they don't engage with the Black community in the city. I've also been to an art gallery and been followed by the security. Art galleries aren't a place that I go to if I'm curious: I go to my friends, I go to music, but I don't go to galleries for that. I think we must address the racism first, and only then can we look at how we can unlock curiosity and build those relationships. I think that is the biggest thing.

JADE MONTSERRAT

So, understanding our colonial and imperial histories is intertwined with recognising how racism works in the UK, and, in a way, that actually does depend on a skill, which is being able to sit in a room and train, learn a new language, an anti-racist language.

MAURICE CARLIN

I think when we talk about language in the context of institutions, we tend to think that we're talking about written language, titles, information panels, and so on. I think that's quite telling, because it assumes that there isn't going to be someone there to have that conversation with you, to be interested in you so that you can be interested in them. I think that how we speak and spoken language is equally as important as written language, because spoken language is also a marker of belonging. If I hear someone who sounds like me, then I'm going to feel more like I belong in that institution.

CHLOE AUSTIN

An audience member has asked the following question: 'Is there even a possibility that this painting exists outside of a frame of racism, the representation of this Black actor on stage in Britain in 1826?'

MAURICE CARLIN

When Sonia Boyce worked with the portrait of Ira for her *Objects of Obsession* programme at Manchester Art Gallery in 2018, she also brought in other interesting thoughts around masculinity, drag, and performativity. So there are multiple frames through which to view this.

KATE JESSON

I think we can look back to Shakespeare, as well, and the pivotal role he played in how we construct our British identity, which was something that Sonia was also drawing from. But Ira didn't just play Black roles, Ira played all the leading roles, which included whiting up to play the white characters. But he always kept his hands black, because he was always made to feel that he was representing his entire race. He would often speak to his audiences about abolitionism straight after his performances. It's also interesting that Ira was much loved in the regions but was never acknowledged in London. This is kind of fitting with the idea that Tate Britain can't quite bring themselves to call their painting *Ira Aldridge* because London could never quite bring themselves to acknowledge Ira either.

And back in the day, to be nationally recognised, you had to be in London – only London could offer you an 'official' theatre experience.

JADE MONTSERRAT

Is that replicated in the London-centric way our art world works now?

AMBER AKAUNU

I guess the reason why we, as *ROOT-ed*, only focus on the north west of England is because there seem to be more opportunities for people of colour in London. Whilst obviously there are more people of colour in London, the fact that there are galleries and theatres that have Black directors is crazy to us, because that doesn't happen up here. It just shows that there's a lot more to do in the north west and it's really interesting that this is where Ira was working.

CHLOE AUSTIN

We have another question: 'In what ways might galleries and institutions confront their racist pasts and presents?'

JADE MONTSERRAT

I keep advocating for widespread racial justice training, but I don't see that as just exclusive to galleries or institutions. I also advocate for places like the British Library or the British Museum being 'occupied' and used as a space where we can redress the history of racism, in a way that is led by people of colour. I think galleries and institutions can confront their racist pasts and presents with new collecting policies, and by listening. There are groups continually bringing it to the attention of these organisations and galleries that this racist past is being perpetuated in the present. It hasn't stopped, so institutions might confront their racist pasts by conceding their sort of 'know-it-all' power.

AMBER AKAUNU

I would say the first thing in addressing the racist past is just being honest. A lot of galleries claim that they care and that they want to address racism in the gallery space, but if they really did care I think they would have done it by now. A lot of us, as Black artists, discuss this all the time and I feel like we have the answers collectively, but galleries don't even approach us. So then we go on to make our own spaces like *ROOT-ed*, we go on to create our own safe spaces because we don't have that in existing galleries.

RIVCA RUBIN

I would love to see a lot of space and time created for engaging in conversations and acknowledging, rather than running away from our racist history and present. Someone has written here that 'colonial history can be covered up and obscured and obstructed using language, institutions are skilled at this'. One way to respond to this is by taking time and having the conversations. It could be really good to learn how to have conversations that avoid people just saying, 'Well, I'm not racist. It's not me. It's the past. It's other people, it's people before me, it's the other generations, I've got nothing to do with this.' I think acknowledging our complicity is really, really crucial. There's a lot of unacknowledged pain, and there's no way we can move forward easily until past and present pain is acknowledged rather than swept under the carpet. That's what I would love to see: institutions actively working to make that happen.

MAURICE CARLIN

I agree that a great place to start is to apologise. Somehow, I think we find it difficult to apologise for the wrongs of the past, but it's necessary as a way to clear some space, in order to begin to engage with curiosity about the present. I don't think that's possible without an apology, or an acknowledgement of the wrongs of the past.

NIKITA GILL

Kate, in the past you've discussed the idea that we try to address decolonialisation, without first addressing colonialism.

KATE JESSON

Yes. It's another problematic word, decolonialisation, and I've learned that it's a white word. I feel a little bit like I slept through the whole chapter on colonialism, because what we're taught, what we know, and what we understand means we are missing huge parts of our histories. I call these 'uncomfortable truths', and throughout this project it's been about how we can use language to shift an uncomfortable truth into a shared truth, really. We're doing lots of research here at Manchester Art Gallery to try to track the money that built the Gallery and bought the artworks. And obviously, in Manchester, in exactly the same way as in Liverpool, our wealth came from the movement of immigrants to our city to turn it into the manufacturing or industrial capital of the world.

CHLOE AUSTIN

There's another great question: 'What about institutions' use of iconography, and how they sell certain exhibitions to Black folks, like 'fraudulent Blackness' as a marketing tool?'

FAUZIYA JOHNSON

That makes me think of when Amber and I did a shoot for Liverpool Hope University for this alumni thing. We didn't realise where our images would be going, and then for the clearing admissions picture on Hope University's website, it was just me! And I do not represent that university whatsoever. Institutions like to 'represent diversity' (or so they think) by putting people of colour and minorities there very visibly.

JADE MONTSERRAT

I was thinking about this idea of selling certain exhibitions to Black folks and wondering whether that's linked to the idea of having frank conversations about racist pasts and presents. The exhibition *Soul of a Nation* (2017) and Kara Walker's *Fons Americanus* (2019) at Tate were really important, but it feels like we're sidestepping our own histories in the UK and we've continued to sort of homogenise with an American identity. High and low culture meet there in quite a violent way. I tie the idea of 'fraudulent Blackness' as a marketing tool to a sense that I had of myself as 'fake Black' in my formative years, because I was clearly someone other than myself to other people. And that also shaped my voice, so when I first went to university, I had this sort of existential crisis whereby I couldn't locate myself in my voice. I didn't know who I was, because I've gone through all these different sorts of education environments, so I'm interested in this idea of 'fraudulent Blackness' as a marketing tool.

KATE JESSON

I was just thinking about apologising and how I tell my kids that saying you're sorry is about not doing it again. I'm not quite sure whether we're ready to apologise in that sense of not doing it again. Also, the archives that cultural institutions hold in relation to the history of all those works. Ira's archive, in particular, tells the story of racism across cultural institutions and the wider thinking that was going on at that time. So there's a relationship between being lost in a cultural collection and being lost within a wider society. I am a great believer that if you can break the cultural institution, then you can start to break other institutions too.

RIVCA RUBIN

I think 'sorry' is rarely meant, and we could move away from the idea of 'sorry'. People put out statements on social media 'oh, we're sorry'. Are they really thought through, felt and meant? And what does such an apology aim to achieve? To make us feel better about ourselves? In my experience mediating conversations, it's more about recognising and accepting that all these things have happened and are happening. It's about acknowledging the other person's and peoples' consequent experiences, loss, pain and anger. Then healing can take place. Then mutually desirable actions can be agreed. Then we can dismantle the systems that our 'forefathers' and-mothers have created, that we white people have and still benefit from. It is then that we can begin to build new structures.

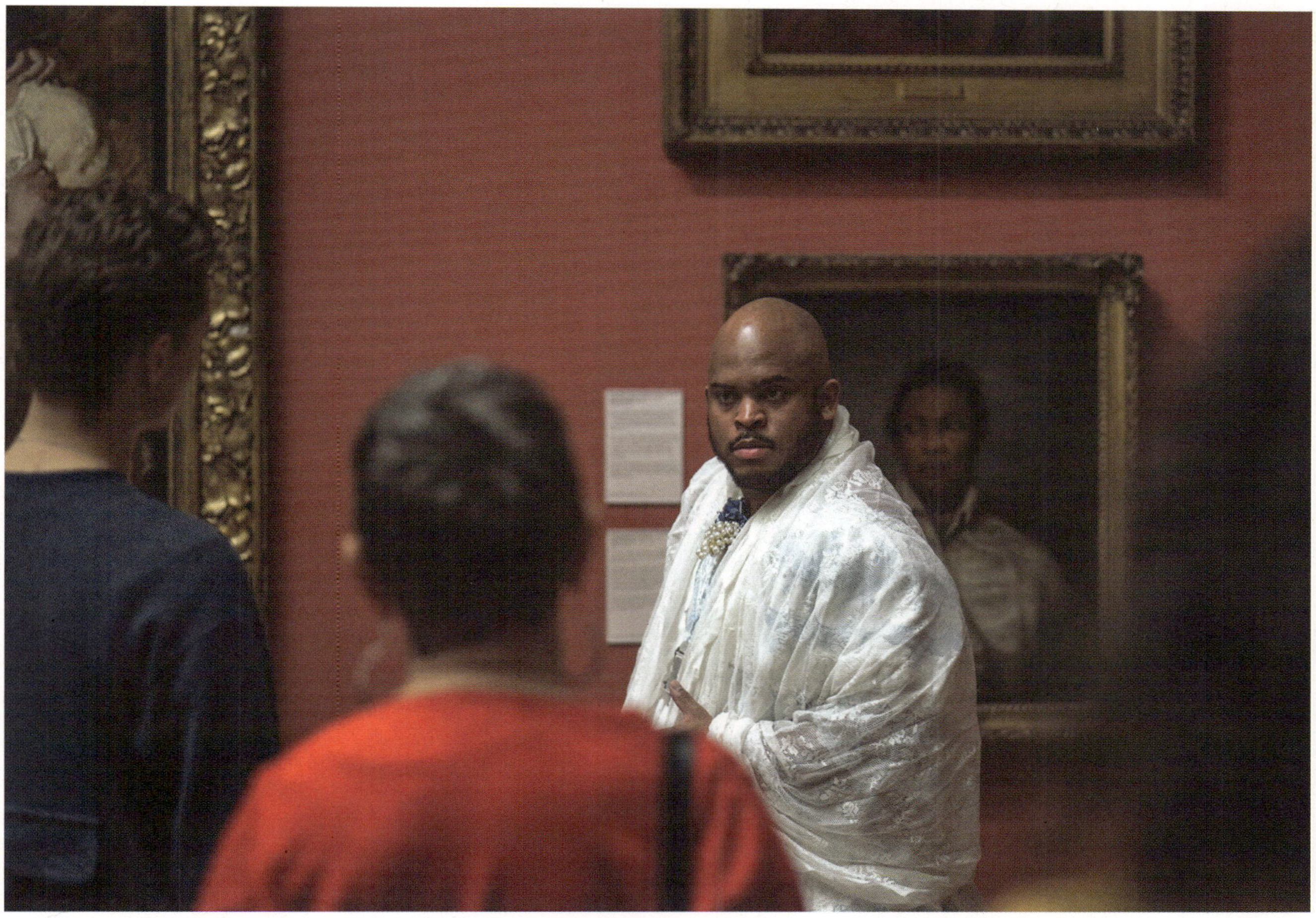

Lasana Shabazz performance at Manchester Art Gallery during the making of Sonia Boyce, *Six Acts*, 2018.

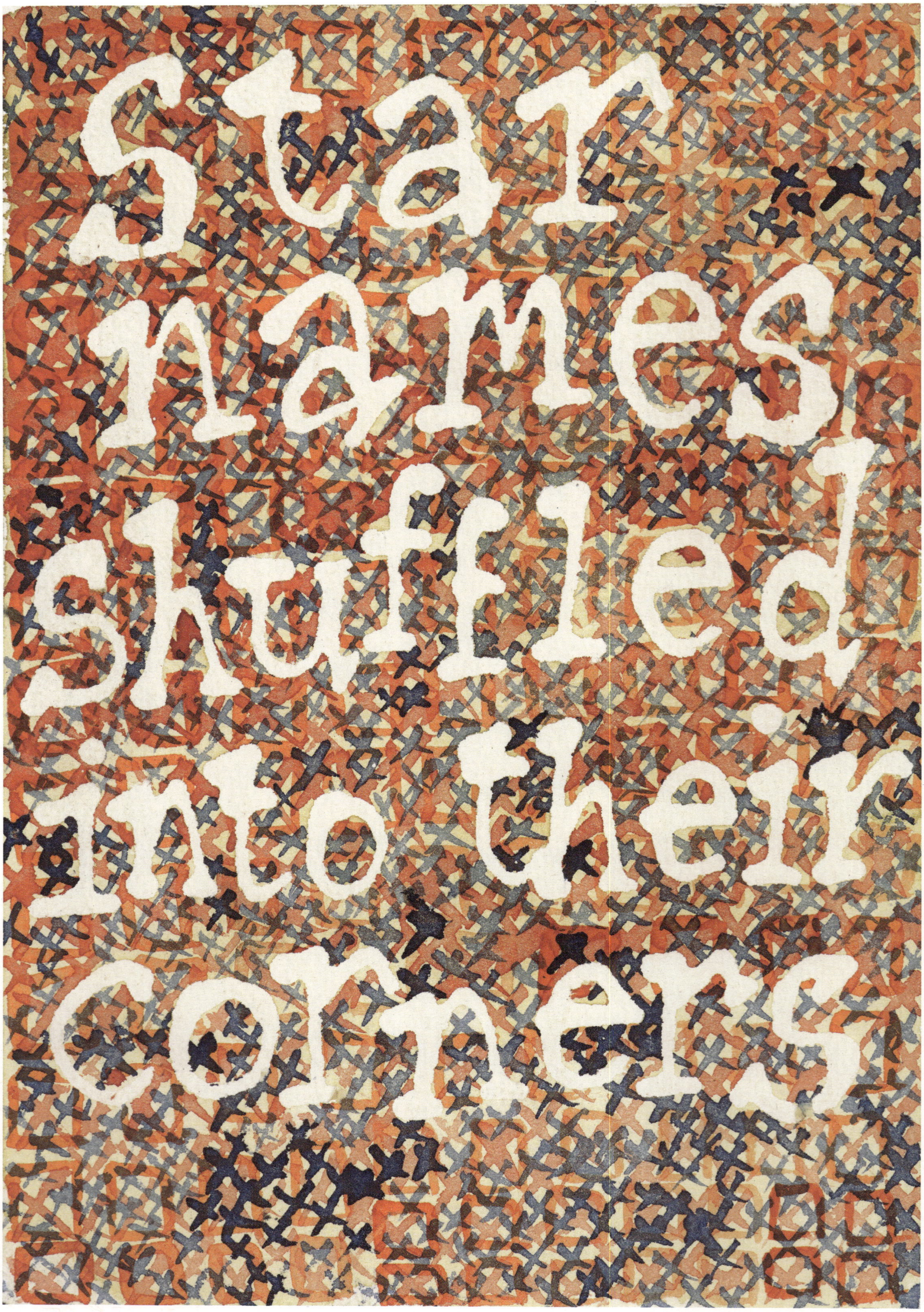

Star names shuffled into their corners, 2021

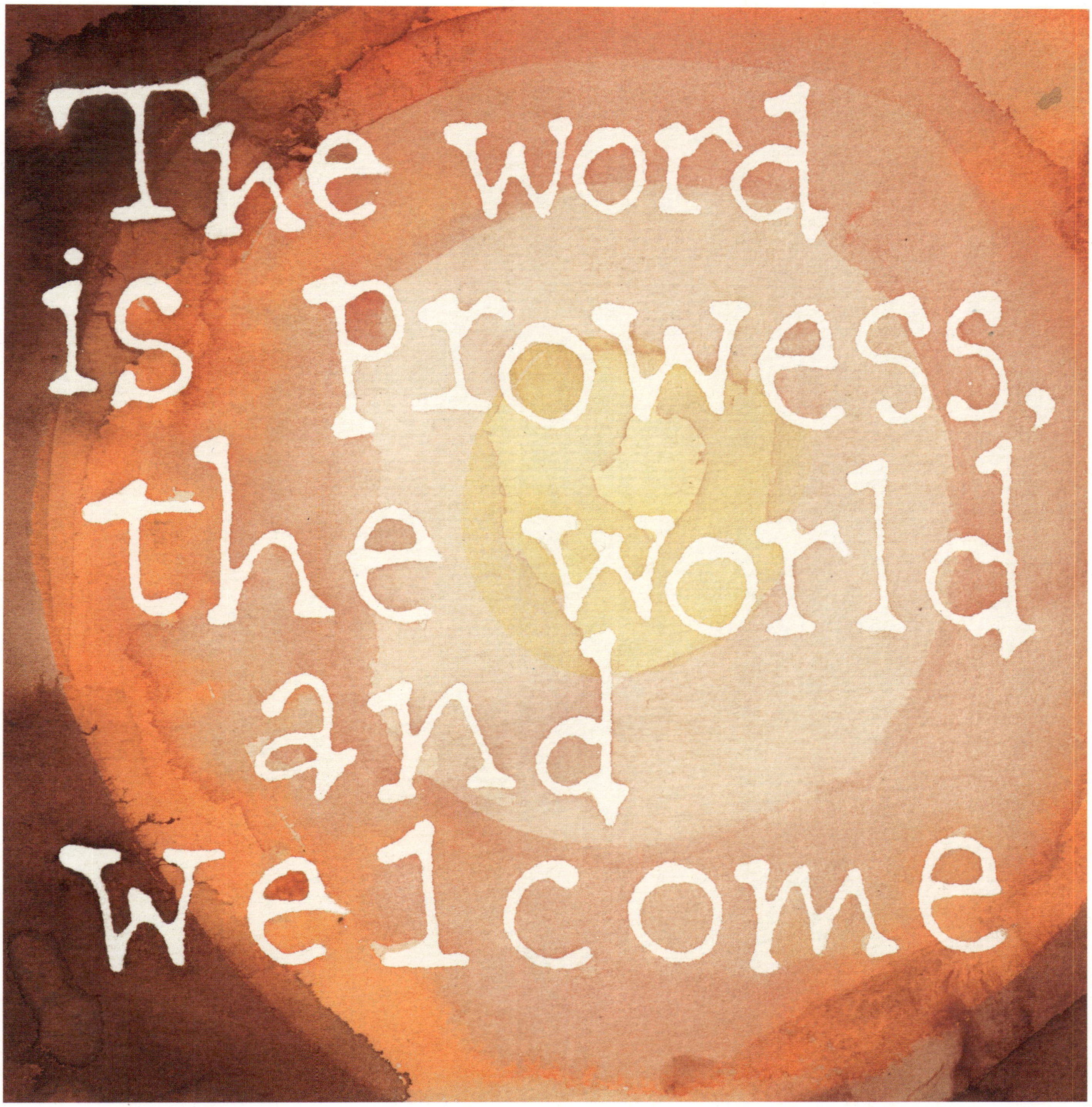

The word is prowess, the world and welcome, 2021

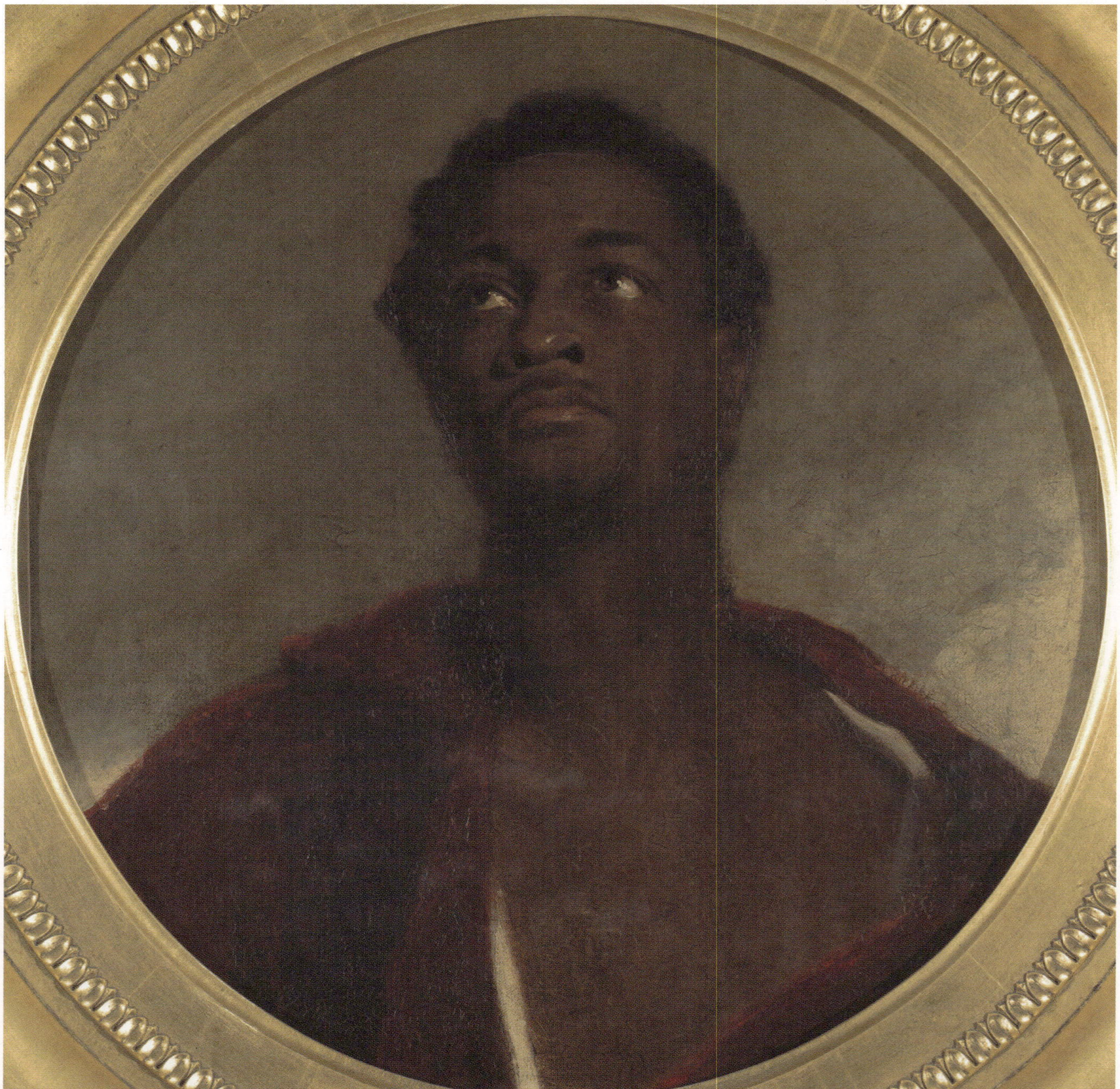

Head of a Man (?Ira Frederick Aldridge), exhibited 1827, John Simpson, Tate, London

IN CONVERSATION

KATE JESSON AND SANDY NAIRNE

This conversation between Sandy Nairne, writer, curator, and former director of the National Portrait Gallery in London, and Kate Jesson, curator at Manchester Art Gallery, took place as part of an online Ira Aldridge study day, hosted by iniva on 27 May 2021. The discussion focussed on the starting point of Jade Montserrat's research for her *Future Collect* project: James Northcote's 1826 painting of the African American actor Ira Aldridge, *Ira Aldridge as Othello, The Moor of Venice*, which was the first work acquired by Manchester Art Gallery. The discussion explored the history of the painting, the historical context in which it was made and acquired, as well as the context in which it currently exists within Manchester Art Gallery's collection.

SANDY NAIRNE

Tell us what is known about the acquisition of this painting for the Manchester collection.

KATE JESSON

In a nice, neat and tidy version of history, we refer to this painting as the first work ever bought by Manchester Art Gallery, so the start of our public collection. Manchester Art Gallery began as the Royal Manchester Institution (RMI). In May 1827, before the Institution was built, the RMI held its first temporary exhibition in the city, called *The Exhibition of Pictures by Living British Artists*. The painting was purchased from this first exhibition with surplus funds raised from ticket sales. So that's when, where, and how this painting was bought.

But *why* was it bought? There are multiple versions of this story. For many years it has been described by Manchester Art Gallery as follows: 'It is thought that the Institution's decision to buy this portrait may have been influenced by Manchester's support for the abolition of slavery in the United States.' What's key here is 'it is thought': we have never been certain about this. When and why was a connection made between the supposed sympathies of the RMI Committee members and this purchase decision?

Who was making the decisions? Who held the power? One could become a Governor, a Hereditary or Life Governor, by paying for the privilege. Underneath the Governors sat a committee of at least 24 elected council members. They had the governance. It was their choice to purchase this painting. Ongoing research as part of our *Whose Power on Display?* programme has produced no evidence to support this version of the reason it was purchased. What I think you have instead is the Gallery retrospectively aligning itself with Ira Aldridge's anti-slavery message with which he finished many of his performances.

Another version of the story of why it was bought is that the RMI must have been commemorating Ira's first performance in Manchester in February 1827, at the Theatre Royal. When we checked the August 1827 committee minutes, so we could be more certain about the original acquisition decision, we found that, in the opinion of the committee, 'it was the best executed painting in the exhibition'. When the governors held their General Meeting in February 1828, they summed it up slightly differently and I feel this is the crux of it, really. They said, 'The purchase was a compliment, considered by the committee to be due to the estimable artist for his patronage of the Institution.' So, I propose that from the outset it was only ever about the artist, James Northcote.

In 1882, when the RMI building and its collection were transferred to the Manchester Corporation, it became the City Art Gallery (now Manchester Art Gallery), so the RMI's first acquisition became the start of Manchester's public collection, too.

SANDY NAIRNE

In the years between 1827 and 1882, I am very aware that Manchester, as well as being a growing centre for empire and industry, was a place of exhibition, producing the *Art Treasures* exhibition in 1857. There is an interesting link here, because the curator of the art section of that great exhibition was George Scharf. Originally an artist, he reinvented himself as a curator and spent part of the 1850s going round all the houses and stately homes of England, persuading the owners to lend their paintings to hang in Manchester. Scharf engineered an incredible assembly of paintings, but by the time of the exhibition, he was appointed as first Director of the National Portrait Gallery in London. He had a very particular interest in creating an institution, a portrait gallery, which would focus on paintings but much more centrally on the subjects, on the people depicted. Shall we move on to the question of founding portraits?

KATE JESSON

Yes, because the National Portrait Gallery's founding portrait has a similar story behind it to ours.

SANDY NAIRNE

In June 1856, Lord Ellesmere got up in the House of Lords, knowing that there had already been discussion in the 1840s about whether a National Portrait Collection or National Portrait Gallery might be formed. He said that if this institution was formed, he would give to the nation his great portrait of Shakespeare, known as the Chandos portrait. When the institution was founded, he did. So that's why the Chandos portrait is the National Portrait Gallery's founding portrait. There isn't any conclusive evidence of who painted it, or when, or whether Shakespeare sat for it.

What also intrigues me is that the trustees were debating who they were going to have in this collection, which figures from history would be there. They were also thinking about authenticity. What has always been in my mind about Shakespeare as 'Number One' at the Portrait Gallery was that this was exactly what they needed, because Shakespeare was a self-made man. Rather than starting with a portrait of an aristocrat or a queen or a king, their first portrait was somebody who had made himself. The idea that Shakespeare made Shakespeare was absolutely riveting to the trustees, because what's in the National Portrait Gallery's DNA is a certain moral and inspirational dimension – about what anybody might be, what anybody might become.

Let's go back to the Aldridge painting and Manchester, because I want to ask you about its different titles. As I understand it, the naming of the portrait was not fixed.

KATE JESSON

Yes, in the same way that Shakespeare's portrait is referred to as the 'Chandos portrait' because of its former ownership by the Duke of Chandos, Ira Aldridge has been absent from his portrait's title too. It takes 157 years before he is recorded as the sitter for this painting. It is recorded in Northcote's notebook from 1826, when it was painted, as *Head of a Negro in the Character of Othello*. Aldridge isn't yet the honoured actor he later becomes. He is described as destitute and on the verge of returning to America. A year later, when the RMI comes to exhibit it, it is called *Othello, the Moor of Venice*.

In the first collection catalogue published in 1846, all reference in the title to Othello is removed and the portrait is known simply as *A Moor*. With this new title permanently attached to the frame, it goes on display in the RMI's first collection exhibition.

It's not until 1983, courtesy of research by drama author Ruth Cowhig, that it is categorically proven exactly who the sitter is. She also shed some light on why Othello may have got lost along the way. She suggests the RMI may have been prompted to dissociate the portrait from the Shakespearean character due to Samuel Taylor Coleridge's 1811-19 Shakespeare lectures. Coleridge questioned Othello's Blackness, suggesting that a 'moor' can be a noble military hero unlike a 'negro'.

After Cowhig identifies Aldridge, he is always mentioned in the label as the sitter, but not in the painting's title. Ira himself had lost his name because whilst performing in the early years, establishing his reputation, he was not referred to as Ira Aldridge. When he performed in Manchester he was billed as the 'African Roscius'. Though his name was not on his playbills for his early performances, his name was certainly known by the time he returned to Manchester. Yet it appears that no connection between the actor and the painting was made. Fast forward to March 2020 when we changed the title again, hopefully for the final time, to *Ira Aldridge as Othello, the Moor of Venice*.

SANDY NAIRNE

Very good. You just need to make sure that it doesn't get changed again. This serves to emphasise the importance of documents around paintings. With the Chandos portrait, Shakespeare doesn't leave us a letter or a diary entry saying something like, 'I went to Mr. Taylor's studio on Friday afternoon,

I wish he'd finish that damned portrait.' That would be perfect because then everything would be tied up, but there's nothing. We miss such things and must work around it.

KATE JESSON

It's also important that we reveal this expanded history and we don't tidy it up. And, of course, ours isn't the only portrait of Ira, is it Sandy?

SANDY NAIRNE

There is a version on loan to the National Portrait Gallery, which we were able to borrow from a private collection during my period of directorship. I was very keen that this version should be brought in to be seen in the collection. It's not the same, it's a copy version. There would only ever be another version because of demand. It's as simple as that. Somebody else wanted it and would have asked Northcote's studio for another version. We don't know whether that was because of the admiration of Northcote or, more likely, admiration of Ira Aldridge. I don't think we know when this version was painted. Maybe someone else does. Anyway, what I wanted to add was this sense of it becoming a question of demand.

KATE JESSON

That's very interesting. There are other possible portraits of Ira, too. There is one at Tate Britain as part of their *Walk Through British Art* display. It has a question mark in the title: *Head of a Man (?Ira Frederick Aldridge)* by John Simpson. It's got an interesting connection to ours that still needs to be explored. It was first shown as *Head of a Black* at the British Institution in London in 1827, the same year that we exhibited and purchased our portrait. It was originally exhibited as an anonymous figure too. Another interesting connection, I think, that could help us better understand what was going on, is that they link their painting to a larger subject painting called *The Captive Slave* of the same year, which shows what they describe as the same sitter manacled to a bench. When this was exhibited in London in 1827 it was accompanied by the anti-slavery poem *Charity* by William Cowper. I think there's more to unpick here.

SANDY NAIRNE

Part of that unpicking could also be interesting because Robert Vernon, who presented the portrait to the Tate in 1847, was a well-known collector of British art. He was one of those collectors who was trying to bring together British paintings and British artists and forming an idea of a British School. If it was also British subjects and this was associated with abolition, it would be very intriguing if there was a link there.

KATE JESSON

That's exactly what the RMI was trying to do, establish a school of British art.

SANDY NAIRNE

Yes, you were ahead of the game because you started in the 1820s when, in London, the only thing that had just started was the beginnings of The National Gallery.

KATE JESSON

Another painting is *Ira Aldridge as Othello*, circa 1830, by Henry Perronet Briggs, which also has an interesting provenance because actor and theatre manager Sir George Alexander sold it to the Garrick Club in London.

SANDY NAIRNE

The Garrick was famous for collecting theatrical portraits. That's why the Garrick would have been a buyer: it has one of the greatest collections of theatrical portraits.

KATE JESSON

And the Garrick was responsible for a resurgence of interest in Shakespeare. It then got sold to National Portrait Gallery Smithsonian in Washington DC, US, in 1972.

SANDY NAIRNE

Why did the Garrick sell it? Do we know why?

KATE JESSON

No, to be continued...

SANDY NAIRNE

The Garrick has done a lot of good work on its records and may have records that explain why it was sold. One even wonders whether they got some other picture of Aldridge instead, whether they did a kind of upgrade and found something else of Aldridge for their collection. Anyway, that would be interesting to find out.

KATE JESSON

I'm also interested because the US appeared to reclaim him in the 1970s. He was unable to be a Black actor in America, and he died a British citizen. There's an uncomfortable feeling around belonging that I'd like to understand more, too.

So, as we speak, there are multiple portraits of Aldridge on display in major public art institutions in England and the US. The act of repetition is a way to both learn and remember something. Yet Ira is still not at the forefront of many people's minds. I know that the National Portrait Gallery in London has prints of Ira, so there's also repetition by reproduction that more people have access to.

SANDY NAIRNE

Yes, there are several. Again, this is an extension of that question of demand. So, Kate, as you say, that question of repetition and multiplicity is also economic. The print market was very extensive. It had developed in the eighteenth century and extended in the nineteenth century. The National Portrait Gallery's print of *Ira Aldridge as Aaron in Titus Andronicus* is typical, and an absolute marker of his fame, because people would have wanted copies and would have been able to afford to buy a print.

There is a story with this print, which is that in 2007, during commemorations for the first Act for the Abolition of the Slave Trade in 1807, there was some terrific work being done by historian and activist, Oku Ekpenyon. Ekpenyon had got on to The Old Vic theatre in London, where Aldridge performed on quite a number of occasions, explaining very clearly why they ought to mark Aldridge's place in their history, and suggesting that they do this with an image of him. She then came to me and asked if a copy of this print could be presented to The Old Vic by her and others who had organised this. I said that the answer was, of course, yes. At the inauguration of this print on the staircase of The Old Vic, the guest of honour was the actor Earl Cameron who, as a young man becoming an actor, was given speech teaching by Aldridge's daughter, Amanda. There was this wonderful sense of linkage back to Aldridge, not being so far away. So, this print has done a lot of good work.

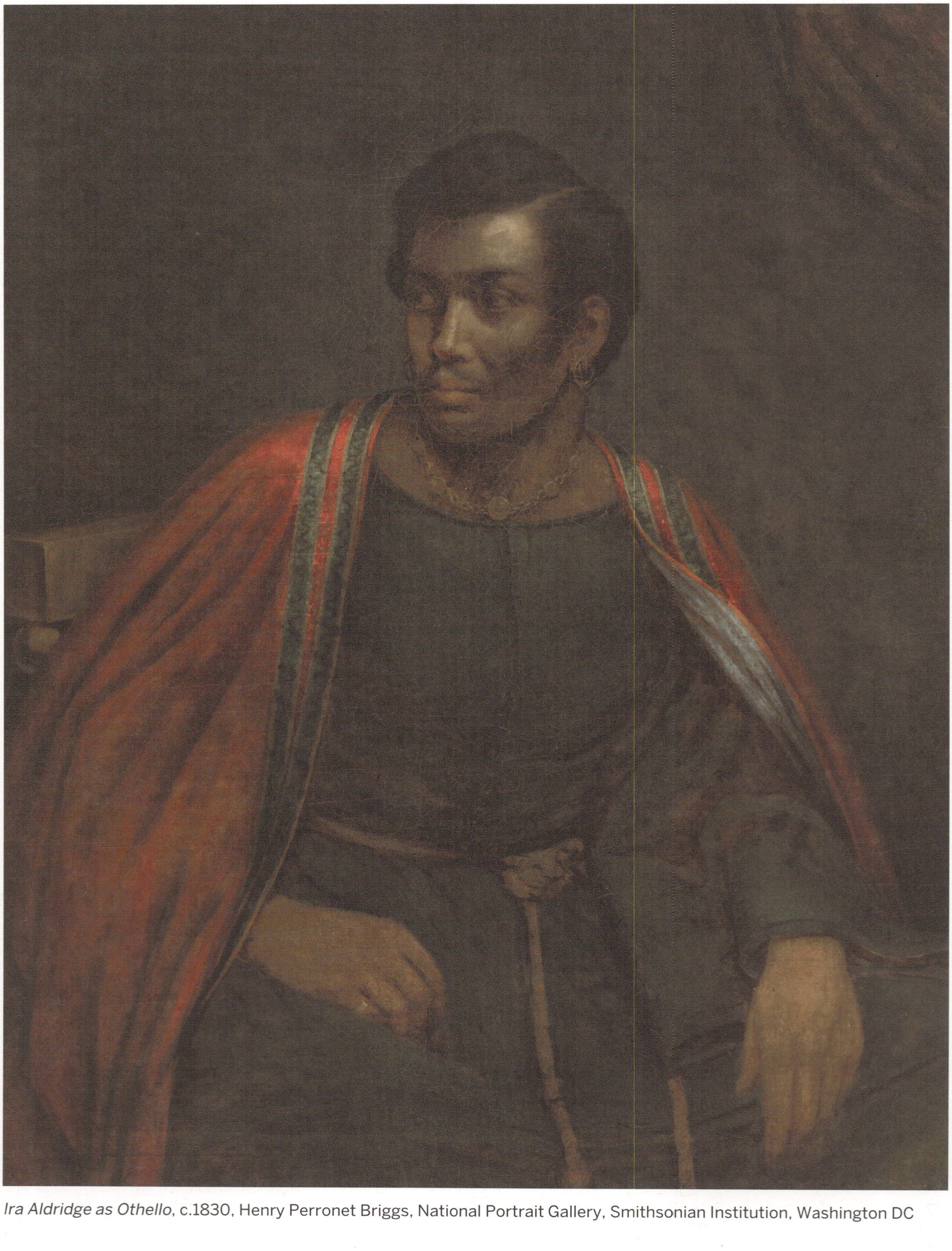

Ira Aldridge as Othello, c.1830, Henry Perronet Briggs, National Portrait Gallery, Smithsonian Institution, Washington DC

ACT II

SCORING PERFORMANCE

Scoring Performance was a conversation between artists Jade Montserrat, Jack Ky Tan, and Amy Lawrence, which took place online on 16 December 2020. Moderated by Nikita Gill, the discussion explored what it means to score a performance. Making connections between everyday performativity and structured theatrical performance, the contributors considered how the performing body and a language of gestural notation might inform the drafting of documents and the implementation of organisational policy. This extract of the conversation centres around the failure of institutions to perform to their 'scripts', the performance of whiteness, and the possibilities of the manifesto as an alternative score for rewriting the function of art institutions.

JADE MONTSERRAT

I was thinking about the multiple meanings of the word 'score'. I just remembered Bessel van der Kolk's 2014 book *The Body Keeps the Score*, and I'm thinking about that as another inroad into the word. We've been talking about keeping to a script, keeping to a score, and how the institution sticks to a script that maintains the institution and serves the institution. I was thinking about how my own body has responded to the conditions we are working in within these systems. My body sometimes seems to respond involuntarily, like I'm carrying the weight of it, whether or not I'm conscious of that. Our bodies are so affected by these sorts of repetitions, I suppose *institutional* repetitions, and I'm thinking about how these tallies are being taken.

JACK KY TAN

I think institutions like having a script and they like having one that *looks* good. But institutions don't necessarily perform the script that they have written. Some institutions think that having the script means they are performing the script. Some institutions will have an equality and diversity script and think that just having it is enough. I mean, I used to do that all the time when I was studying for exams: I just thought if I photocopied enough, then I would do well. I thought having the textbook meant that I was a good student. Same thing with institutions: they've got the performance score, but they're not actually performing it. They're not embodying it. How do you get them into that point of embodiment?

If you want to perform a score, you get off your arse and move, don't you? So the organisation needs to get off its organisational arse and just start moving, at the very least. Most organisations think the work happens in the boardroom, in governance, but governance is really just like score writing. At some point, that writing of the score needs to be translated into organisational performance. I also think of organisations as a body: they have a body. If we're thinking about how a dancer moves, how does the organisation move?

JADE MONTSERRAT

You asked a beautiful question before: how can we make the body of an organisation perform differently and not just pay lip service? How can the white gaze identify the white gaze? How can an eye look at itself? That's the potential that

I'm hoping we can develop. But it's more than an artwork or performance, it's something else, isn't it?

NIKITA GILL

That brings us onto another question, which is: how does one identify the absences derived from lack of care, or the lack of emphasis on care in policy, or policy construction?

JADE MONTSERRAT

We've spoken before about 'the void', and the idea that once you've identified the absence, you don't necessarily have a language to speak about it. And if you do have a language to speak about it, have you got people to listen, who *want* to listen to what you've got to say?

JACK KY TAN

I was talking about it in terms of filling a recruitment vacancy in an organisation. How does an organisation decide that it needs a new staffing role, for example? How do you decide that you need a new programme curator or a new marketing assistant? I originally trained as a potter, and pottery is all about not making the pot but making the void. It's about sculpting a hollow ready to be filled. It's about crafting the void and understanding the shape of the void that you want, and then what will eventually fill it.

When an organisation tries to fill a void, I think they often just go, 'Yeah, we need a marketing director,' or, 'Oh, we need a senior marketing communications person, because every other organisation has one, so we have to have one too.' But what if we thought of the organisation as vessel, and tried to find out what kind of void we need to fill in that organisation? Then the question becomes, 'What's the shape of the communications voice in your organisation, specifically?' And then it's about really learning to feel the sides of that space. If you feel that space better, you will understand that the void is an active and positive emptiness. So then you're more careful about how you describe the emptiness and how you invite people to fill it.

JADE MONTSERRAT

I was wondering if, without that specificity, filling the void often becomes a case of comparison or competition?

JACK KY TAN

Yes. For example, the idea that 'every organisation has a CEO, so we need a CEO'. Twenty years ago that meant: 'We need a CEO, and that means an older, white, middle class man by default, because that's the void we had in our heads.' Now I think, okay, that's how it used to be but how can we rethink this? Maybe we need three CEOs, maybe it should be a job share. It's about learning what works for you, rather than taking something straight off the peg, or swallowing whole organisational formats that come from outside your community, your organisation, or your cosmology. It feels like, in the arts, we're just taking on wholesale commercial hierarchies that come from the Chicago School of Business, or Harvard, or some other market-oriented form of management inappropriate to the work and values of the arts, social and charities sector. We recreate these hierarchies within art institutions and make them look like neoliberal businesses. Is that really how art works, or how that specific art organisation works for that community? Maybe we should be working out how to carefully describe other forms of void or organisation, so that we can craft them differently.

AMY LAWRENCE

I often think that a lot of arts organisations would benefit from having more of a commercial model, in some senses. I've worked with a lot of organisations who have no HR department, no culpability, no process for grievance, and no actual, functioning financial department. There are no procedures in terms of care or management because they've often developed from a more DIY approach without infrastructure, or they're very low on budget so they operate with a skeletal team. When you were talking about the void I was thinking about skills audits. When a board is looking for a new member, often a 'skills audit' is conducted: the board asks what skills it needs and then looks for people with those skills. I've recently had conversations about whether lived experience of having a protected characteristic is a skill. I think this is a really interesting conversation, because it is a skill if it's completely lacking in the current dynamic of the space. There's a whole viewpoint and perspective missing, but I think that's where there's friction, because it's not considered a skill by the institution. So you have a lot of organisations at the moment looking for people who are Black, Asian, or a racialised minority in the UK, but out of fear of looking tokenistic they are not clearly stating this, and instead are still advertising these roles via the skills audit format. There's something kind of sticky about that because it makes you wonder what kind of situation these new board members are coming into.

JACK KY TAN

Maybe commercial is the wrong word, but I think having some kind of thoughtfulness about what is needed in an organisation is important. Being thoughtful about your communications, being thoughtful about your complaints process — as thoughtful as you would be if you were making a work of art. I think a lot of organisations don't do that, including artist-led ones, so I completely agree with you about that. But up until recently in the commercial model (and by commercial model, I mean the traditional model that you'd see in management consultancy and what they think the ideal organisational structure is) they would not have included having embodied Black and Asian experience as an essential part of that model. The commercial model lacks a lot of things that I think are quite important because it's all about business and not about empathy. Things like empathy and care, which are not normally identified as skills, should be recognised. For me, it's about looking to other inspirations for models, rather than the Anglo-American optic of what a model should be. One stumbling block, for example, with global ethnic majority arts organisations, is when they're suddenly given a tonne of money and asked to grow. For some reason, they think they ought to grow into the likeness of European white organisations, because white modernity and its aesthetics has credibility and further fundability. So they start putting in white structures with white key performance indicators and something gets lost along the way. We should be more diverse about how we inform our governance or our performance scores.

AMY LAWRENCE

We've also spoken about how the manifesto could be seen as a score, which links to these thoughts around organisational structures. Just as a disclaimer, there are a lot of DIY arts organisations that have incredibly good ecologies of care and are actually much better than large organisations, but often there's a missing dynamic of having a board or governance structures. But I was thinking about manifestos and how they might relate to scores and structures. I've been looking at the theatre scholar Larry Neal's Black Arts Movement manifesto from 1968,[1] which is American-centric, but it speaks about how Black artists must attempt to achieve a 'Black aesthetic'. He explains that, as Black artists, you should resist becoming an individualistic participant in Western art structures, and it's not something which is available to you. I think that links to what you were saying about funding and shifts towards white models of growth or power that come with funding. But there's something about manifestos, for me, that give a kind of direct instruction. I read a few manifestos — the Fluxus one, the Dada one, and the Black Arts Movement one — and I noticed that they all have a similar structure. There's a recognition of the ideas of their ancestors or peers, then the reason for the manifesto's existence, then the content, and then, at the end, there's always a sense of existential urgency. What if you applied that same urgency to an organisation? What if you created all your policies around that kind of structure? I think there's something in the manifesto as a sort of contract, or a series of ideas for how something can happen or be put into action.

NIKITA GILL

A member of the audience has just asked: 'It's usually important for the CEO, and for all of us, to perform whiteness. What's the score here: PhD? Eton? Oxbridge?'

[1] 'The Black Arts Movement is radically opposed to any concept of the artist that alienates him from his community. Black Art is the aesthetic and spiritual sister of the Black Power concept. As such, it envisions an art that speaks directly to the needs and aspirations of Black America. In order to perform this task, the Black Arts Movement proposes a radical reordering of the western cultural aesthetic. It proposes a separate symbolism, mythology, critique, and iconology. [...] When we speak of a "Black aesthetic" several things are meant. First, we assume that there is already in existence the basis for such an aesthetic. Essentially, it consists of an African American cultural tradition. But this aesthetic is finally, by implication, broader than that tradition. [cont. overpage]

JACK KY TAN

There's a sense in which the employment contract is like a performance score: you've turned up for an interview, but you're not from Eton. You're being interviewed by Etonians or Oxbridge grads and you just don't quite dress right, or you don't speak right, or you can't tap into the same memories as the people interviewing you, or most of the people that you're going to work with in that company. So the performance score is: 'I'm just here to do my job, I'm super qualified to do my job.' And yet there's a meta-performance happening around you, of people who've been to Eton, or been to Oxford, or have their own tribe. So it's a question of how you can succeed in performing that meta-score. And I think we all learn to do that in various ways. Even in the arts, we're all performing a kind of social contract, or a kind of meta-score that's unsaid.

JADE MONTSERRAT

Does this bring us to racial or queer battle fatigue, whereby you're constantly part of this performance that's going on around you? The question is really pertinent to my experience of going to the Courtauld Institute in London. I thought, according to the performance that was going on in my family, that I was just going to do law and go into my stepfather's law practice. But I didn't realise that was really against what he wanted, because he had his own plans with his law firm. So I did history of art, and my art teacher told me: 'You'll never get in, it's only people from Eton and Harrow who go there.' When I got there, I would talk about myself as the token Black person in the class, and I'd laugh about it. It was part of a performance that I didn't fully understand, and I certainly didn't have a vocabulary to speak to it or confront it. So that's 20 years of being dragged through racial battle fatigue, I suppose. We're talking about a normalisation of violence: the idea that we should all assimilate or that we all perform to the tune of our masters is a normalisation of violence. I feel quite strongly that I perform a lot, and I don't even realise it's happening until it's too late, and I've spent the whole time performing on these terms that you're talking about. And then I don't know how to address it because I've been made complicit in the performance already. But I'm so practised at that...it's how I was educated to be.

JACK KY TAN

Even when you're struggling to recover some of the power from 'the masters' (white institutions like the Arts Council, or whoever's funding you) in order to be recognised, you have to perform some whiteness to get your foot in the door, I think. You're so 'other' that they can't even recognise where you're coming from. That performance could be as simple as being 'logical', or not blowing my top and being angry at the injustice I see unfolding right in front of me, which is an outrage I feel all the time but I'm not allowed to be because that's just not done in 'polite society'.

It encompasses most of the useable elements of Third World culture. The motive behind the Black aesthetic is the destruction of the white thing, the destruction of white ideas, and white ways of looking at the world. The new aesthetic is mostly predicated on an Ethics which asks the question: whose vision of the world is finally more meaningful, ours or the white oppressors'? What is truth? Or more precisely, whose truth shall we express, that of the oppressed or of the oppressors?'

Neal, L. 'The Black Arts Movement.' *The Drama Review*: TDR, vol. 12, no. 4, 1968, pp. 28–39.

JADE MONTSERRAT

It also plays into the stereotype that you're trying to avoid. It's already been assumed that you are probably not going to last the course because you are going to get angry, because it's in your nature.

JACK KY TAN

Yeah, so there's this idea of tricksterism or code switching. They're inviting us to be on boards to perform a certain function, but then once you're 'in', how do you unperform, in a way?

JADE MONTSERRAT

We were talking about the room for interpretation in performance art, but there is very little wiggle room in the performance of governance that you're talking about here.

JACK KY TAN

Yes, I think on script institutions say they're anti-racist and anti-sexist. So all you're doing is performing the script that they've asked you to perform. But when you actually try to perform it they hold up their hands in horror, and go, 'Oh my God, this person we've invited is actually going to hold us to account. You actually want us to do what we said we're going to do?' I think that's the issue.

JADE MONTSERRAT

Or even if you just hold up a mirror and say, 'Look, this is a performance,' and explain what's happening, you're bound to fail, in a way, as the minority.

AMY LAWRENCE

I think some liberal or liberal-seeming organisations take a masochistic pleasure in the palatable Black person raising an issue. They say, 'Come and tell us what we're doing wrong. We want to hear it.' There's almost pleasure in understanding failure, but with a very clear boundary. When I think about scores, I think of potential and possibility, I don't think of a set script. For me, the script and the score are very different. The score is possibility and potential and the content can also be changed or shifted, but the script is set and decided. I think with the organisation, you can perform whiteness, or you can also perform a sort of non-whiteness, but anything in between that is difficult. I'm interested in this idea that people who are minoritised or marginalised have this amazing understanding of the oppressor, and the roles and boundaries they set. You need emotional intelligence, a very strong emotional intelligence, to be able to read a boardroom and understand how far you can push certain subjects. It's like a particular sensitivity.

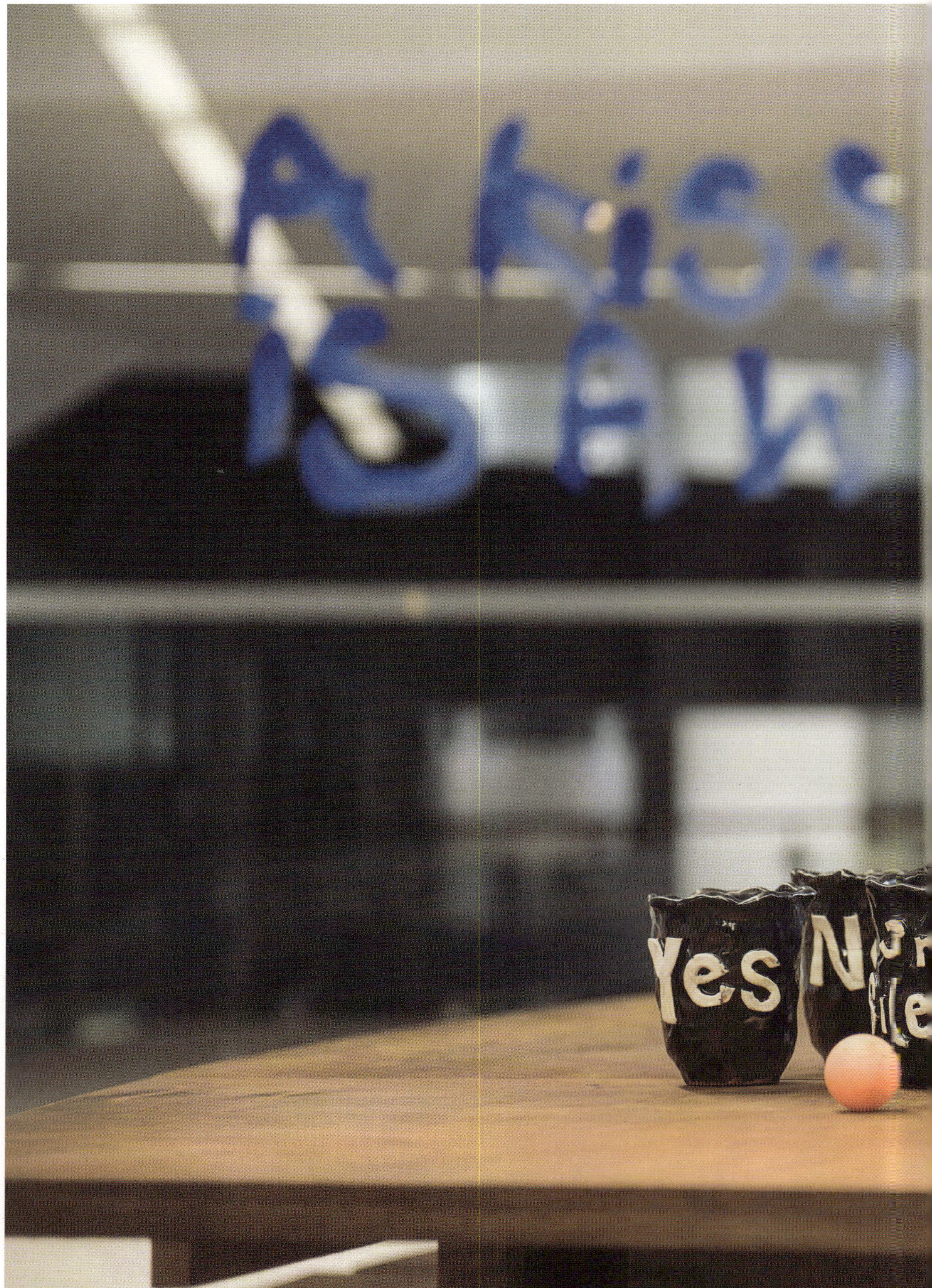

Conference (Decision Pong), 2015, Jack Ky Tan, Performance and installation at the Institute of Contemporary Arts Singapore for the solo exhibition *How To Do Things With Rules*

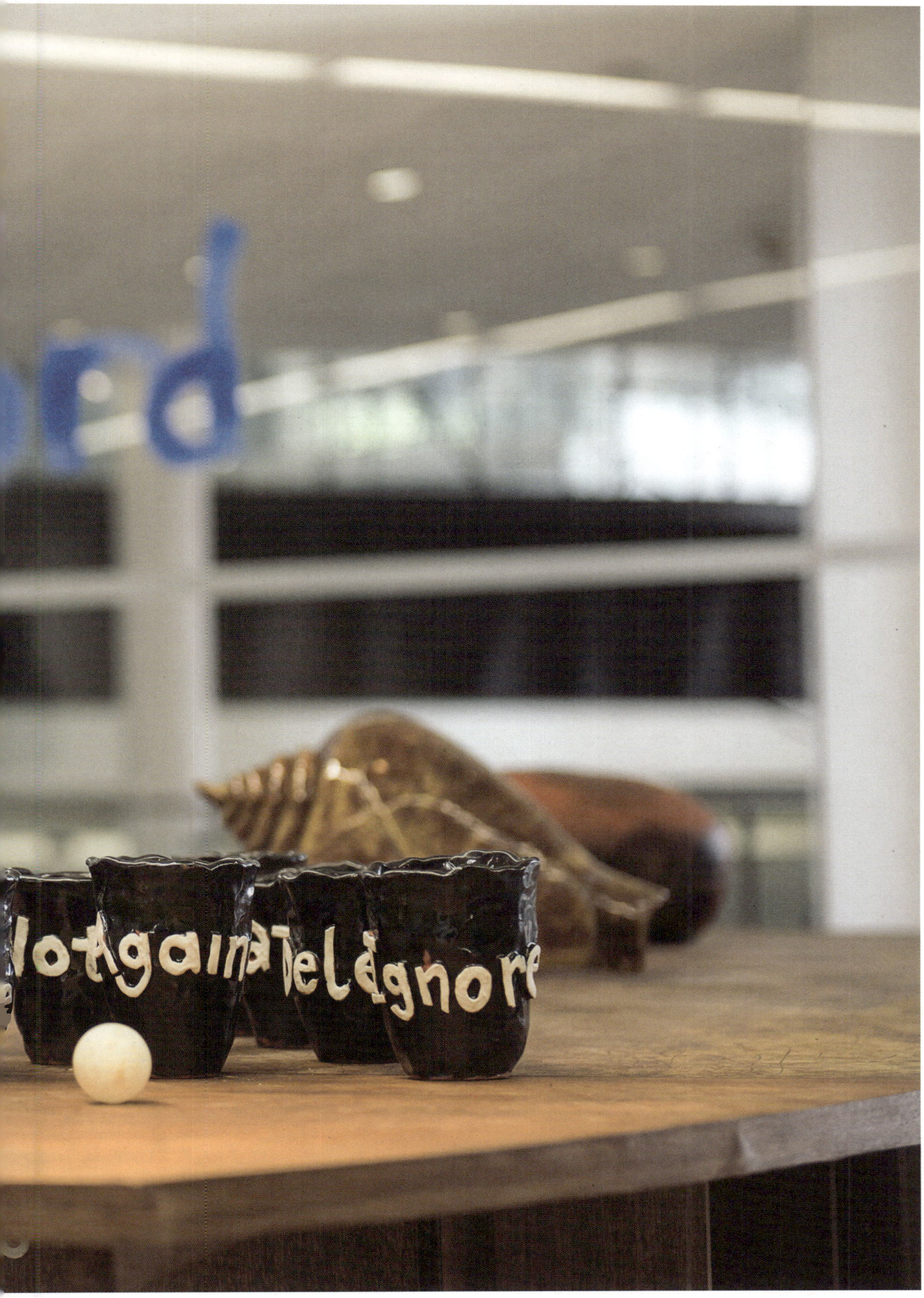

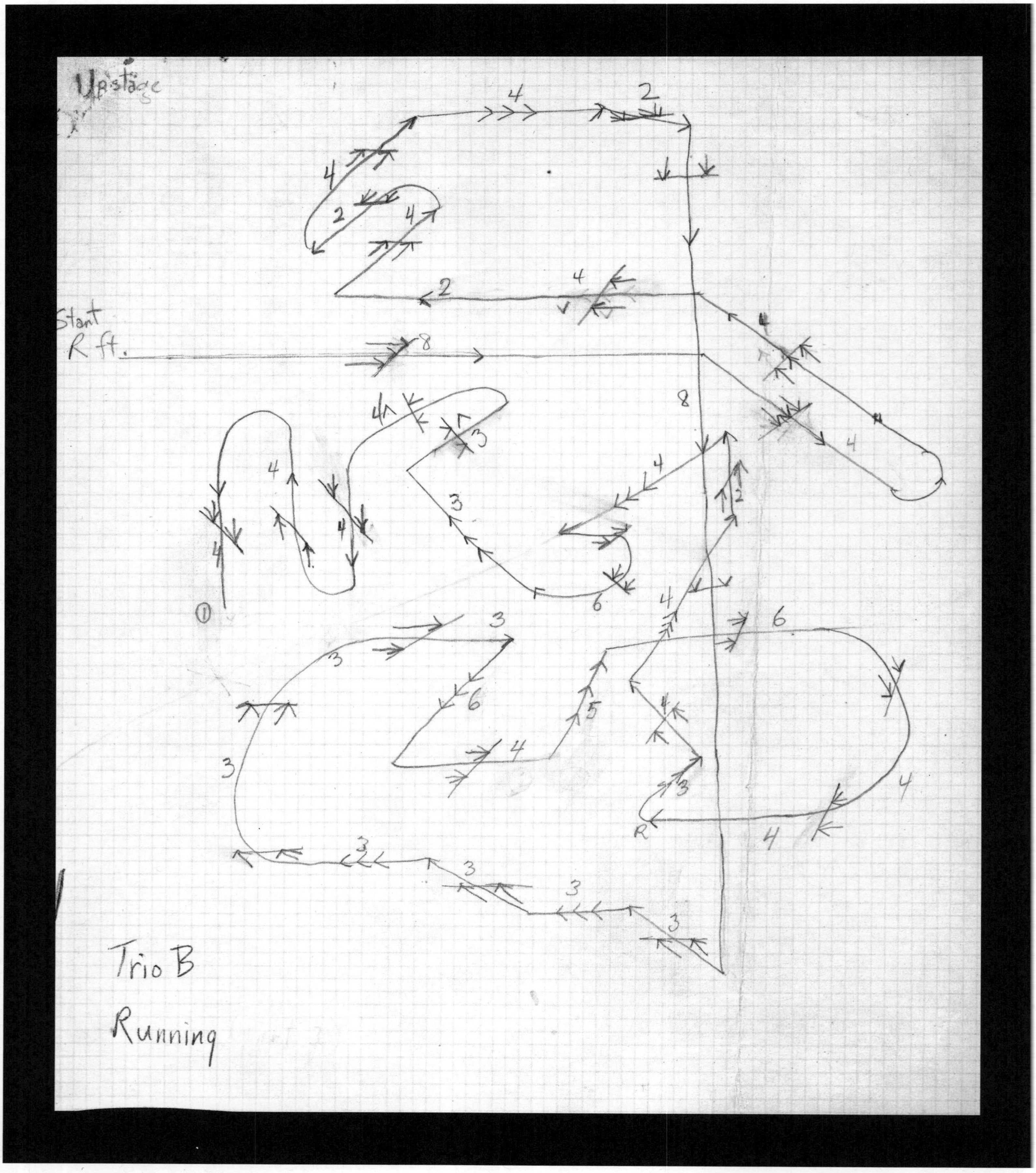

Yvonne Rainer's Score for *Trio B, Running* from *The Mind Is a Muscle*, 1966–68, Getty Research Institute, Los Angeles (2006.M.24)

BLACK PANTHER PARTY

1. WE WANT FREEDOM. WE WANT POWER TO DETERMINE THE DESTINY OF OUR BLACK COMMUNITY.

We believe that Black people will not be free until we are able to determine our destiny.

2. WE WANT FULL EMPLOYMENT FOR OUR PEOPLE.

We believe that the federal government is responsible and obligated to give every man employment or a guaranteed income. We believe that if the White American businessmen will not give full employment, then the means of production should be taken from the businessmen and placed in the community so that the people of the community can organize and employ all of its people and give a high standard of living.

3. WE WANT AN END TO THE ROBBERY BY THE CAPITALISTS OF OUR BLACK COMMUNITY.

We believe that this racist government has robbed us, and now we are demanding the overdue debt of forty acres and two mules. Forty acres and two mules were promised 100 years ago as restitution for slave labor and mass murder of Black people. We will accept the payment in currency which will be distributed to our many communities. The Germans are now aiding the Jews in Israel for the genocide of the Jewish people. The Germans murdered six million Jews. The American racist has taken part in the slaughter of over fifty million Black people; therefore, we feel that this is a modest demand that we make.

4. WE WANT DECENT HOUSING FIT FOR THE SHELTER OF HUMAN BEINGS.

We believe that if the White Landlords will not give decent housing to our Black community, then the housing and the land should be made into cooperatives so that our community, with government aid, can build and make decent housing for its people.

5. WE WANT EDUCATION FOR OUR PEOPLE THAT EXPOSES THE TRUE NATURE OF THIS DECADENT AMERICAN SOCIETY. WE WANT EDUCATION THAT TEACHES US OUR TRUE HISTORY AND OUR ROLE IN THE PRESENT-DAY SOCIETY.

We believe in an educational system that will give to our people a knowledge of self. If a man does not have knowledge of himself and his position in society and the world, then he has little chance to relate to anything else.

6. WE WANT ALL BLACK MEN TO BE EXEMPT FROM MILITARY SERVICE.

We believe that Black people should not be forced to fight in the military service to defend a racist government that does not protect us. We will not fight and kill other people of color in the world who, like Black people, are being victimized by the White racist government of America. We will protect ourselves from the force and violence of the racist police and the racist military, by whatever means necessary.

7. WE WANT AN IMMEDIATE END TO POLICE BRUTALITY AND MURDER OF BLACK PEOPLE.

We believe we can end police brutality in our Black community by organizing Black self-defense groups that are dedicated to defending our Black community from racist police oppression and brutality. The Second Amendment to the Constitution of the United States gives a right to bear arms. We therefore believe that all Black people should arm themselves for self- defense.

8. WE WANT FREEDOM FOR ALL BLACK MEN HELD IN FEDERAL, STATE, COUNTY AND CITY PRISONS AND JAILS.

We believe that all Black people should be released from the many jails and prisons because they have not received a fair and impartial trial.

9. WE WANT ALL BLACK PEOPLE WHEN BROUGHT TO TRIAL TO BE TRIED IN COURT BY A JURY OF THEIR PEER GROUP OR PEOPLE FROM THEIR BLACK COMMUNITIES, AS DEFINED BY THE CONSTITUTION OF THE UNITED STATES.

We believe that the courts should follow the United States Constitution so that Black people will receive fair trials. The Fourteenth Amendment of the U.S. Constitution gives a man a right to be tried by his peer group. A peer is a person from a similar economic, social, religious, geographical, environmental, historical and racial background. To do this the court will be forced to select a jury from the Black community from which the Black defendant came. We have been, and are being, tried by all-White juries that have no understanding of the "average reasoning man" of the Black community.

10. WE WANT LAND, BREAD, HOUSING, EDUCATION, CLOTHING, JUSTICE AND PEACE.

When, in the course of human events, it becomes necessary for one people to dissolve the political bands which have connected them with another, and to assume, among the powers of the earth, the separate and equal station to which the laws of nature and nature's God entitle them, a decent respect of the opinions of mankind requires that they should declare the causes which impel them to the separation.

We hold these truths to be self-evident, that all men are created equal; that they are endowed by their Creator with certain inalienable rights; that among these are life, liberty, and the pursuit of happiness. That, to secure these rights, governments are instituted among men, deriving their just powers from the consent of the governed; that, whenever any form of government becomes destructive of these ends, it is the right of the people to alter or abolish it, and to institute a new government, laying its foundation on such principles, and organizing its powers in such form, as to them shall seem most likely to effect their safety and happiness. Prudence, indeed, will dictate that governments long established should not be changed for light and transient causes; and, accordingly, all experience hath shown that mankind are more disposed to suffer, while evils are sufferable, than to right themselves by abolishing the forms to which they are accustomed. But, when a long train of abuses and usurpations, pursuing invariably the same object, evinces a design to reduce them under absolute despotism, it is their right, it is their duty, to throw off such government, and to provide new guards for their future security.

Written: 15 October 1966
Source: War Against the Panthers, by Huey P. Newton, 1980
Transcription/Markup & corrections: MIM/Brian Baggins
Online Version: Marxist History Archive 2001

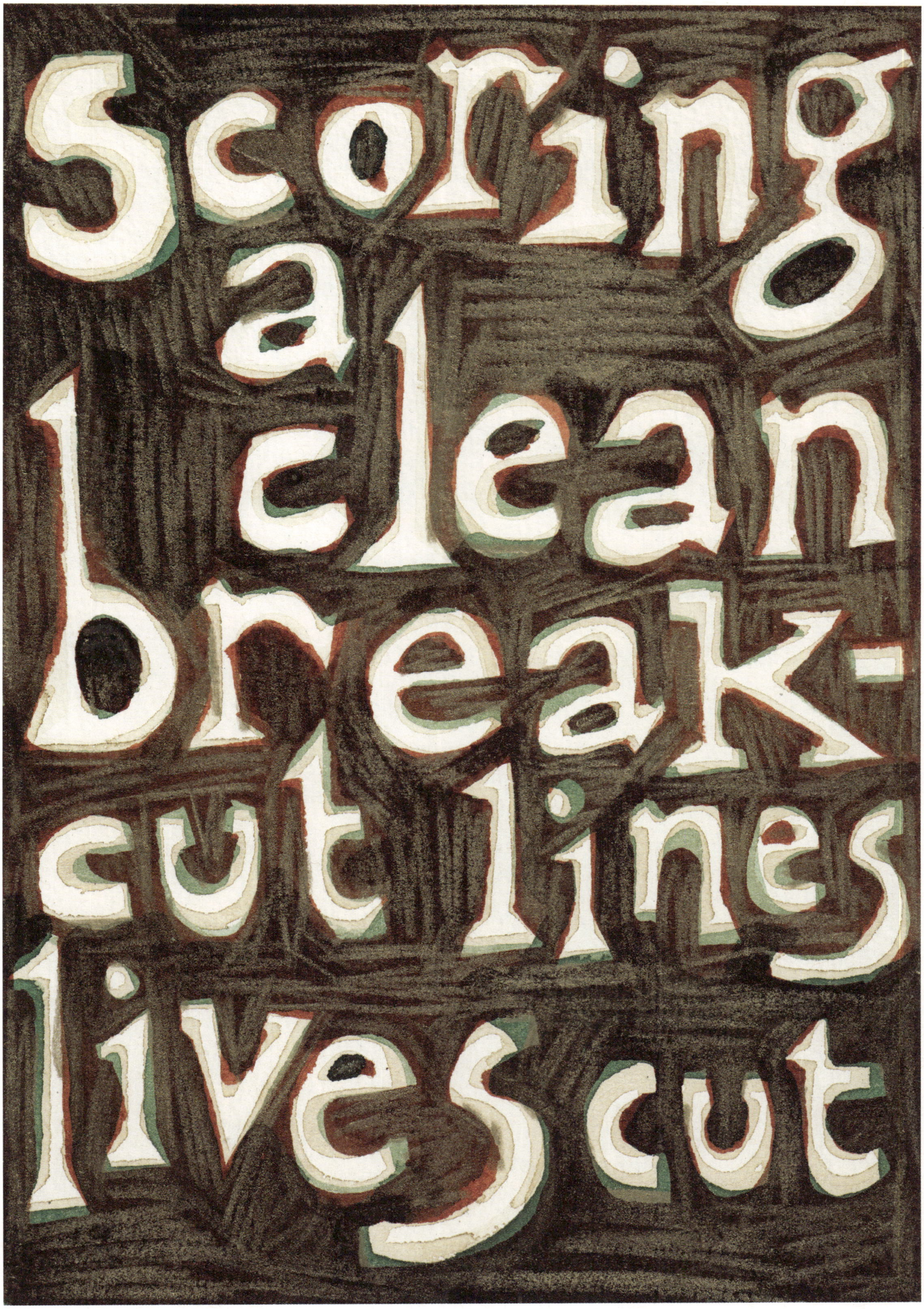

Scoring a clean break – cut lines lives cut, 2021

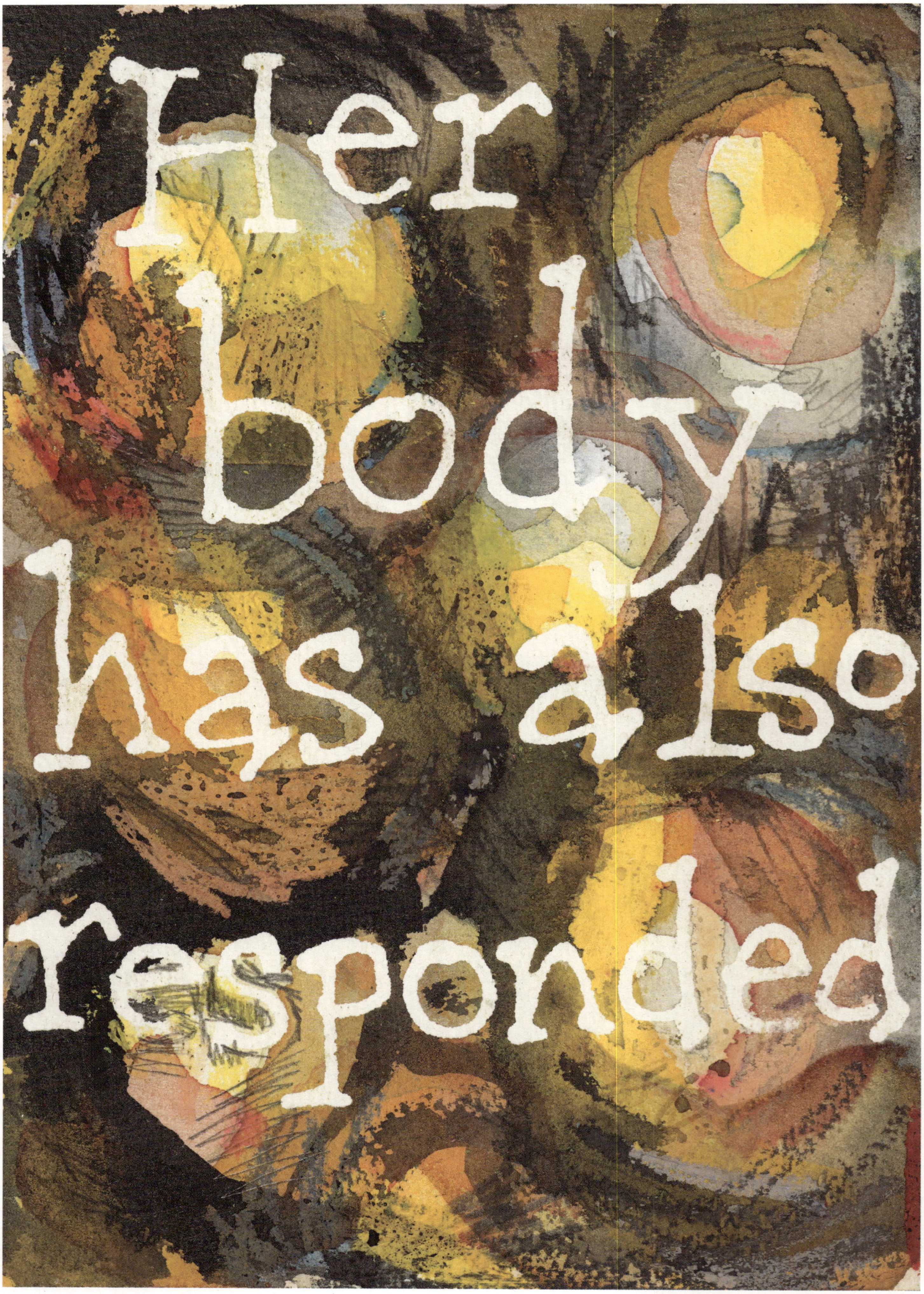

Her body has also responded, 2021

NIKITA GILL AND JADE MONTSERRAT

Jade Montserrat and Nikita Gill met on 3 June 2021, to take stock of their shared experiences working on Jade's exhibition at Manchester Art Gallery as part of iniva's *Future Collect* programme. Their conversation considers their own process of working together with care, the damage done by institutional tendencies to perform optical representation of minoritised artists and workers without the necessary support structures in place, and what it might mean for an institution to 'weigh its words before giving them breath' in that context.

NIKITA GILL

We're going to have this conversation about our project together, which has been quite a wild and exciting ride. I think it would be nice for us to do a kind of emotional audit, and think about the 14-16 months that we've been working together on it. How has it been for you?

JADE MONTSERRAT

I like the idea of an emotional audit, but although our work has been centred on care and an awareness of our emotions, I don't know how well I can talk through the emotional side of the work that we've done. Whilst we've worked incredibly hard, within a particular set of restrictions, we've been working with compassion towards each other and have been receptive and sensitive to each other's needs. By 'restrictions' I mean what's been expected of us as artists and curators working in this first iteration of the *Future Collect* project. Our working process has impacted how the work has been made and how I've felt throughout that, so the work has been made out of that compassion. So, yeah, I'm good. I'm working on the watercolours this month for the final stage of the exhibition at Manchester Art Gallery and I'm also frazzled. I feel like I really haven't stopped since I was frazzled in 2019. So not much has changed for me, except I've got different strategies to be able to keep working at this pace and respond to certain demands.

NIKITA GILL

Yeah, that's definitely true. I think it's also really important to think about this in context with the fact that there are a lot of conversations happening around care at the minute, but there is a disconnect between that and the actual conditions we are all working within. The demand for outcomes, the production of artwork and creativity, seem to have ramped up during the coronavirus pandemic: to perform, to reperform, to develop something. It almost felt as though, during the last lockdown, people needed creativity more than ever to keep going, to rejuvenate themselves, to make sense of things, to unpack their feelings, to unpack the world around them. We were all isolated in a way that we didn't choose for ourselves, but was necessary for the safety of one another. That's definitely been on my mind regarding the work that you did, for example, with the Bluecoat in Liverpool on instituting care. How do you institute care during this period of time? How do you manage the necessity and the capacity to work in such a way that you can keep going?

JADE MONTSERRAT

Yeah, it's evident to me that a lexicon around care has suddenly become popular, but there's a clear dissonance when social care is having to be highlighted by footballers like Marcus Rashford. Or waking up this morning to the news that the government is looking at cutting foreign aid. For me, personally, being in isolation is my default. I grew up in the middle of nowhere, without any neighbours, with very few relations or family or friends coming to my house. There were the three of us: me, my mum, and Joe, who was in my life for 20 years from when I was four and who I eventually called dad. My mum still lives out there; there's only generated electricity and gas lights, so I didn't grow up with terrestrial television. So I came to make art through being in comparative isolation all of my life. I went to boarding school very early on, which was also isolating. You're trapped in a community of sorts, but if you're the only Black child in a school at eight years old, and you're staying there for weeks on end, you're in a very particular kind of isolation. These schools were far away from what I understood as 'home': they are centres of education that foster individualistic thinking. There wasn't an approach to community and care because community was a big C Conservative community, in terms of how class is constructed and the subsequent hierarchies. As a child you don't understand this, so your emotional intelligence and behavioural responses can be out of sync, and are therefore punished.

The cuts to the arts we're seeing now are a further minimisation of society and community, which I understand to be an inherent aim of a Conservative government.

NIKITA GILL

It's interesting, because your isolation came from living away from the city and, conversely, mine came from living in the city. Being the only Black curator in the art gallery space, there are support systems that you don't necessarily know you need until you've already experienced the loss, isolation, or solitude that comes from not having them.

JADE MONTSERRAT

I feel there's been friendship and support between the two of us, whereby some of the unspeakable aspects of the last year have been held just by knowing that we have each other, and we've spoken about that feeling of isolation before. It's a disappointment, isn't it, because you have to work through your position and your emotional response and the precarity that you're faced with. It's incredibly disappointing to know that you're the only person of colour working at that level within the whole of Manchester Art Gallery.

NIKITA GILL

When people look at art galleries or cultural institutions and are able to think of them as a place you go to find safety, a place where you are not othered, that's a privilege. Seeing yourself represented in an art gallery or an institution isn't necessarily just about seeing bodies pictured on the wall that are like yours. Black bodies on the wall is not necessarily representation to me. I think seeing a support system, seeing a gallery assistant I feel I could potentially talk to about the unspeakable, or the shared lived experience of a work, or a different perspective, is representation. Seeing yourself within an institution means things like seeing a talk by a scholar who has information about historic Black lives that you didn't previously have access to, because it's not taught to you in school, you know?

JADE MONTSERRAT

Absolutely, I couldn't agree more. I'm thinking about what you're saying alongside the phrase 'expendable bodies in unspeakable isolation', which appears in one of my works: the idea that you can feel expendable and isolated in these environments by the mere fact of where you're positioned in society, how you're viewed because of intersectional marginalisation and minimisations.

Over this last year we've all been pummeled around. I was working with a local organisation and our relationship broke down precisely because I had raised some of these things we're talking about here. Several weeks after that working relationship broke down, their head curator posted a picture of him picking out his favourite work from a group open call exhibition on their Instagram account. The work he had chosen was a painting of a Black woman, and he admitted that it was his favourite work, but he couldn't say anything about it.

Several other artists and I working with the institution had previously tried to raise a number of issues with him and open up a reciprocal conversation, but it was shut down because of his defensiveness. By posting this image, it felt like he was performing an idea of representation for an audience after having previously shut down our concerns. How do you address that? How do you speak to that? I think that this can compound these feelings of isolation in a museum or art gallery setting, for sure. Those at the top of institutions act as gatekeepers around these conversations.

NIKITA GILL

Yeah, and it also really speaks to the development of your performance *Rehearsal Methods: audition pieces for solo and collective*, which has come out of your practice and all these considerations. There are two specific phrases I'm thinking about from the work, which Performer I (who was played by Alistair Hudson, director of Manchester Art Gallery, in our first performance) speaks to Performer II (who was played by me), who transcribes them onto the wall in charcoal. There was the phrase taken from Shakespeare, and something about things being 'left unsaid'...

JADE MONTSERRAT

'Everything that is said and not heard, said and unsaid.' And the Shakespeare phrase is: 'Weigh thy words before giving them breath.'

NIKITA GILL

Those two phrases have stuck with me since being part of *Rehearsal Methods,* along with 'expendable bodies in unspeakable isolation'. It's interesting, because 'weigh thy words before giving them breath' is a cautious warning from Othello to his friend Iago. I would love to see that turn of phrase reappropriated again, but in contractual policy: when you're in the process of writing a job description, or an opportunity to 'diversify' your work team: that you weigh your words before giving them breath. Meaning that you are transparent with what it is that you are offering, what support you are willing to give, and what space you are committing to supporting your future Black or Asian colleagues who will take over from you, bring in knowledge that you don't have, and share experiences that you can't possibly speak to.

JADE MONTSERRAT

In response to that, I'm thinking about how Ira Aldridge used to use the time after his theatrical performances to address the crowd on abolition issues. One of my favourite phrases from *Rehearsal Methods*, which is made in response to both the context of this last year and working with Ira Aldridge, is: 'The police aren't going to do it, the police aren't going to do it for us, the police aren't going to do it, the police aren't going to do it for us.' I'm trying to incorporate antidotes to stress and trauma within the performance score by having the performers 'chop the wood', which is another breathwork exercise that I learned in yoga, throughout the performance. The Chorus interprets the statement about the police by making a 'nee-naw' noise and the score continues to instruct the Chorus to make that 'nee-naw' noise and 'duh' or a 'doh' sound. That, to me, also speaks about incarceration in parallel to isolation, constraint, constriction. Through these constructions, we're brought back to constricted airways and then being stressed or traumatised just imagining that. So what could I do to counter that? Return to my breath.

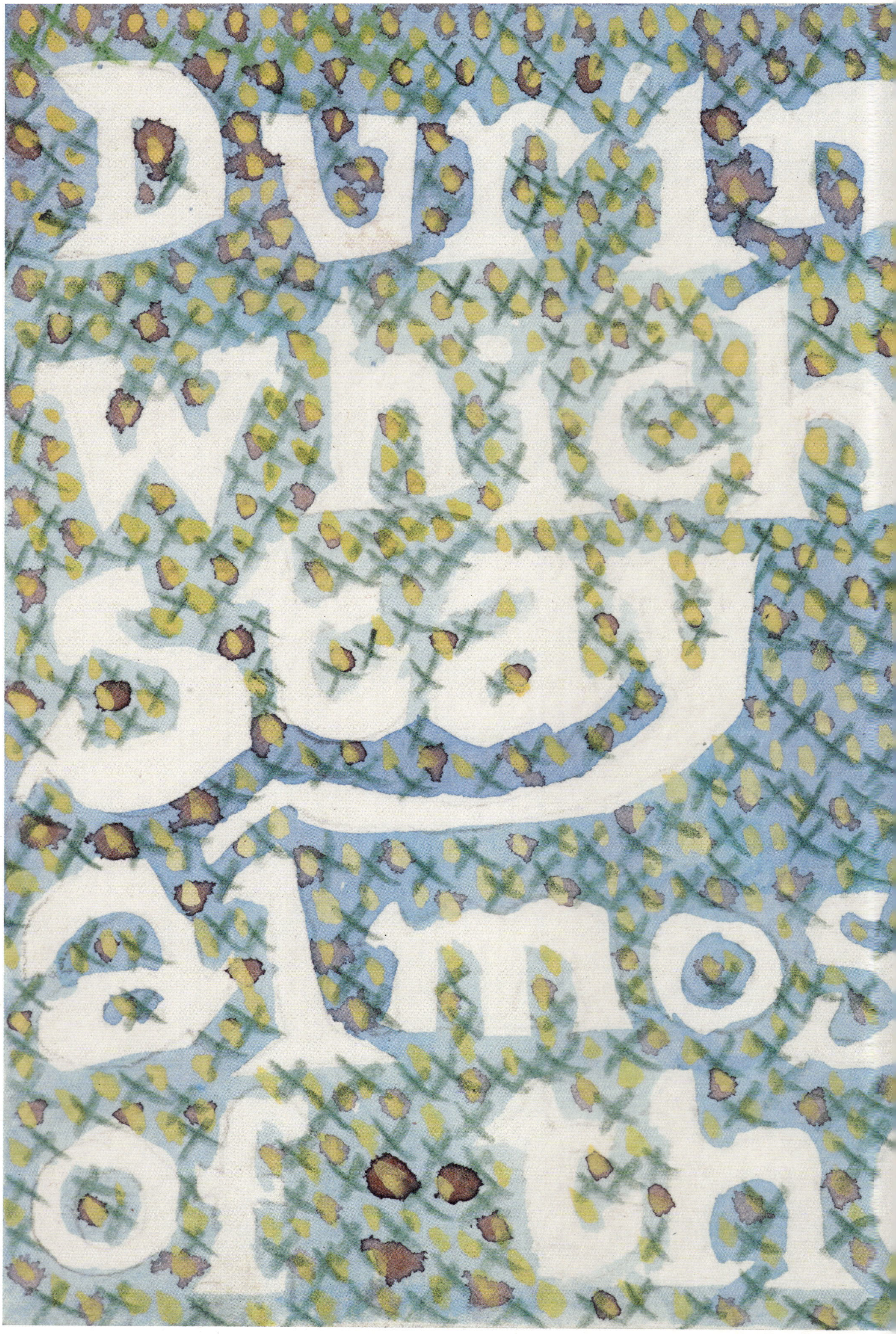

During which I stay home almost all of the time, 2021

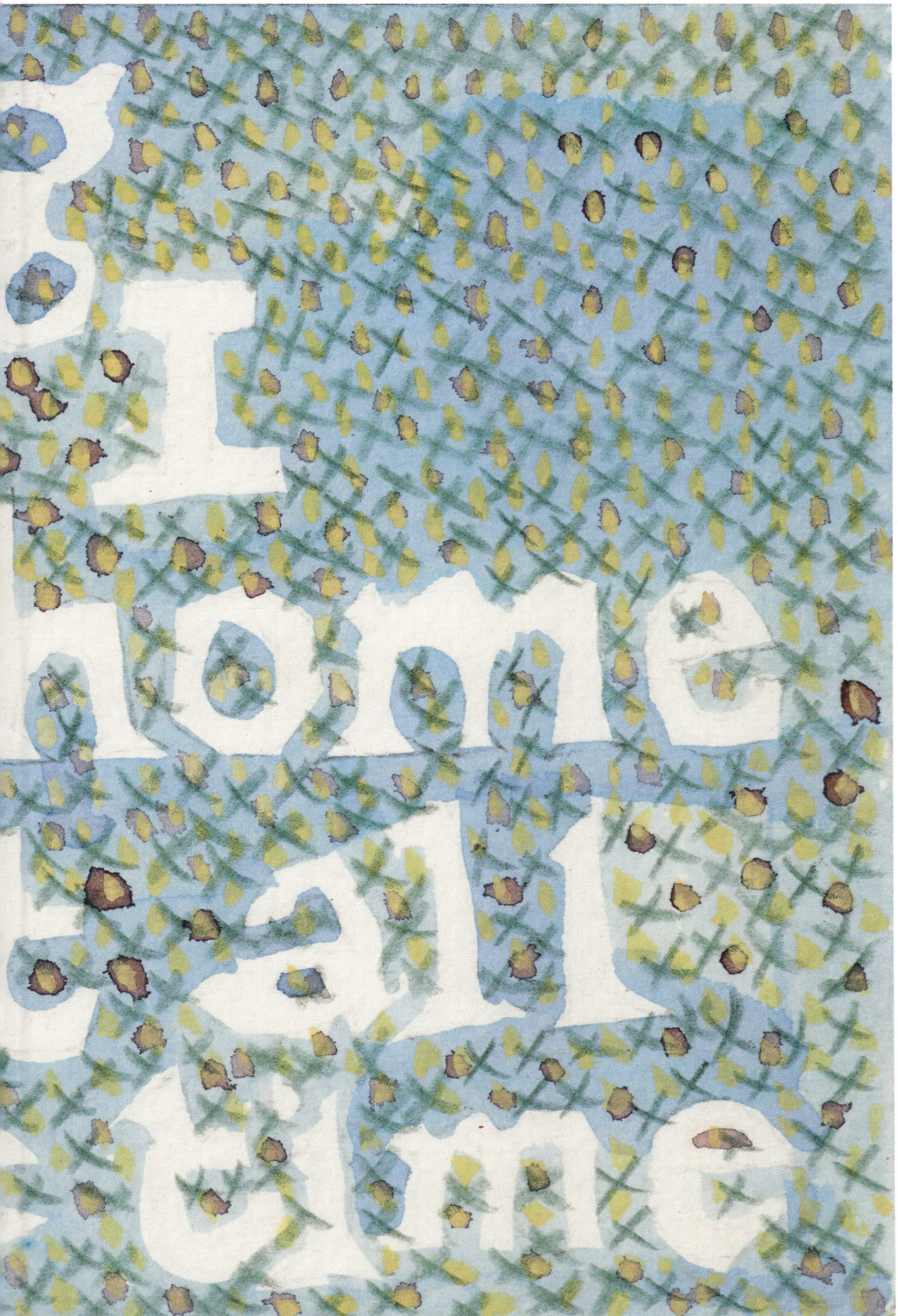
I
ome
time

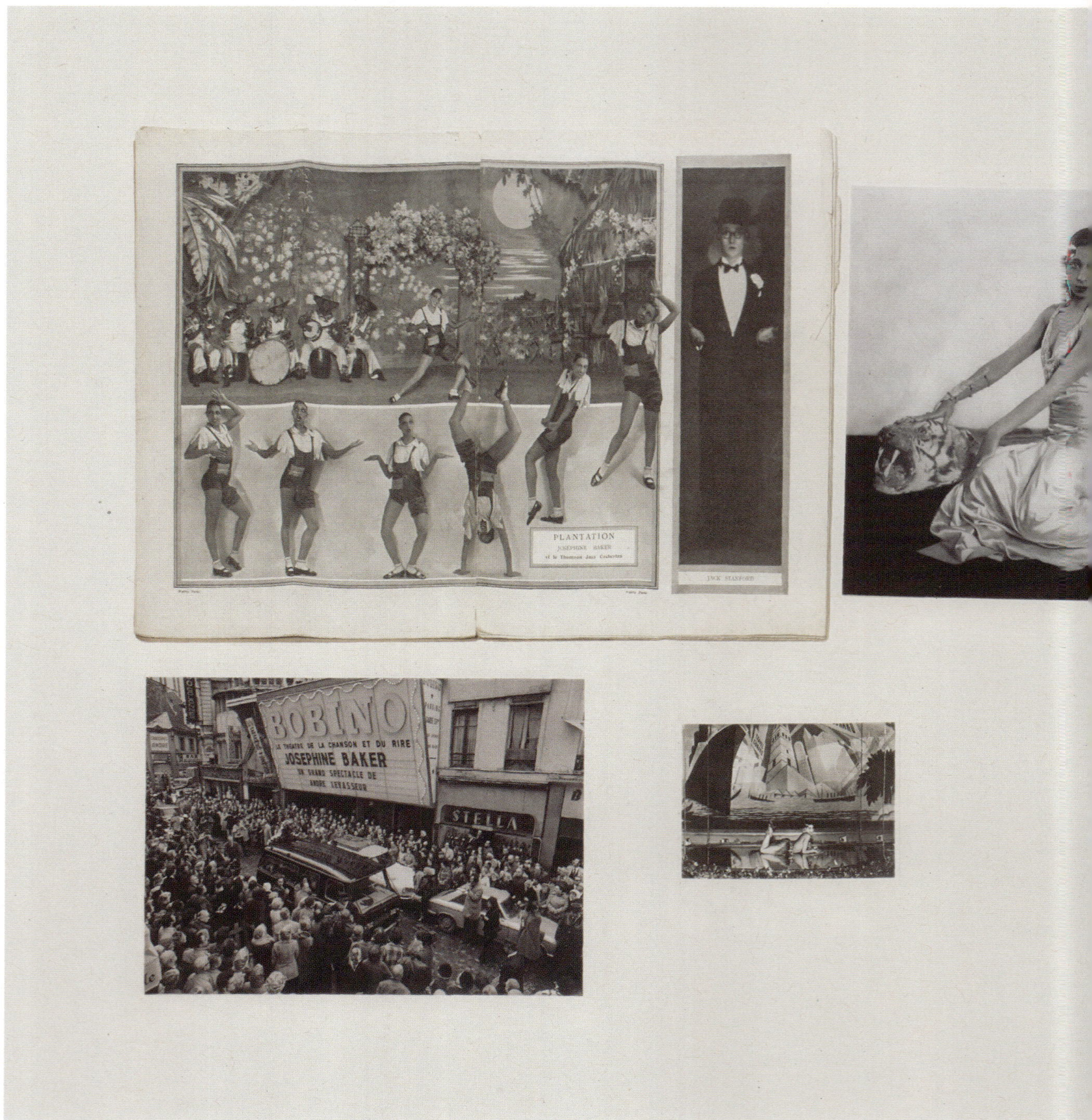

Vitrine view of studies by Jade Montserrat on display in Montserrat's *Constellations: Care & Resistance*, 2020 at Manchester Art Gallery

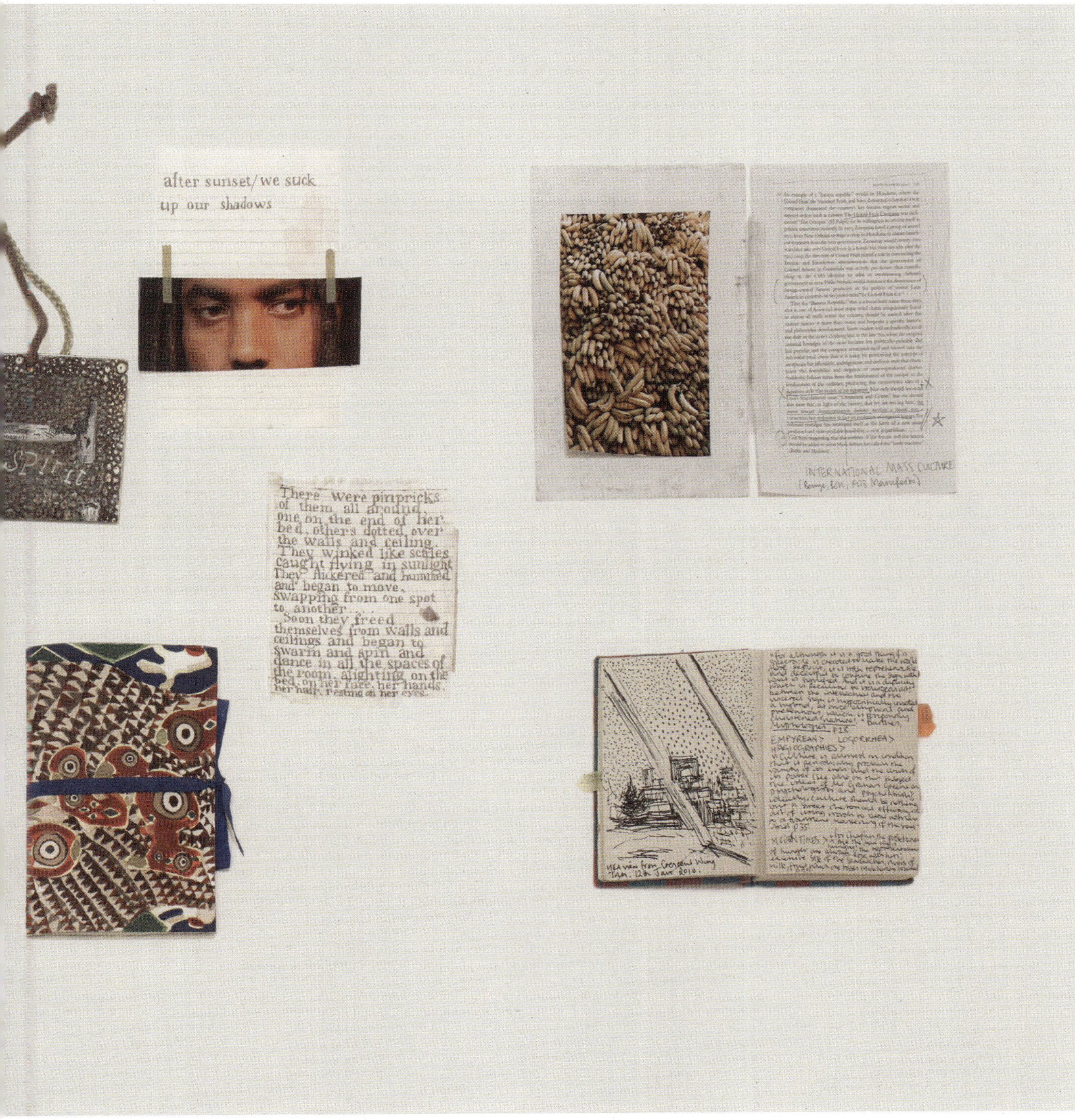
after sunset/we suck
up our shadows
There were pinpricks of them all around, one on the end of her bed, others dotted over the walls and ceiling. They winked like scales caught flying in sunlight. They flickered and hummed and began to move, swapping from one spot to another....
Soon they freed themselves from walls and ceilings and began to swarm and spin and dance in all the spaces of the room, alighting on the bed, on her face, her hands, her hair, resting on her eyes.
INTERNATIONAL MASS CULTURE
EMPYREAN

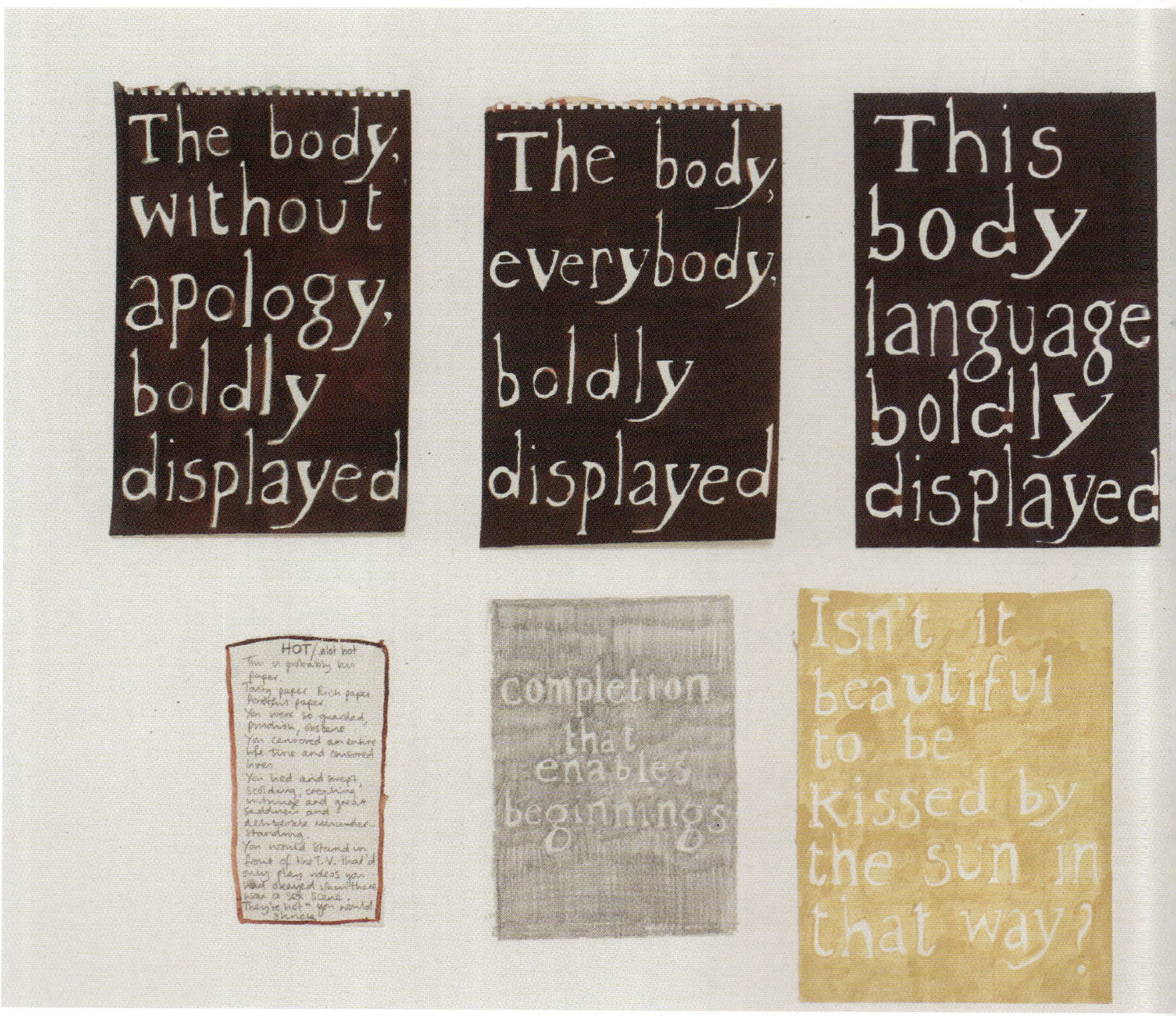

Vitrine view of studies by Jade Montserrat on display in Montserrat's *Constellations: Care & Resistance*, 2020 at Manchester Art Gallery

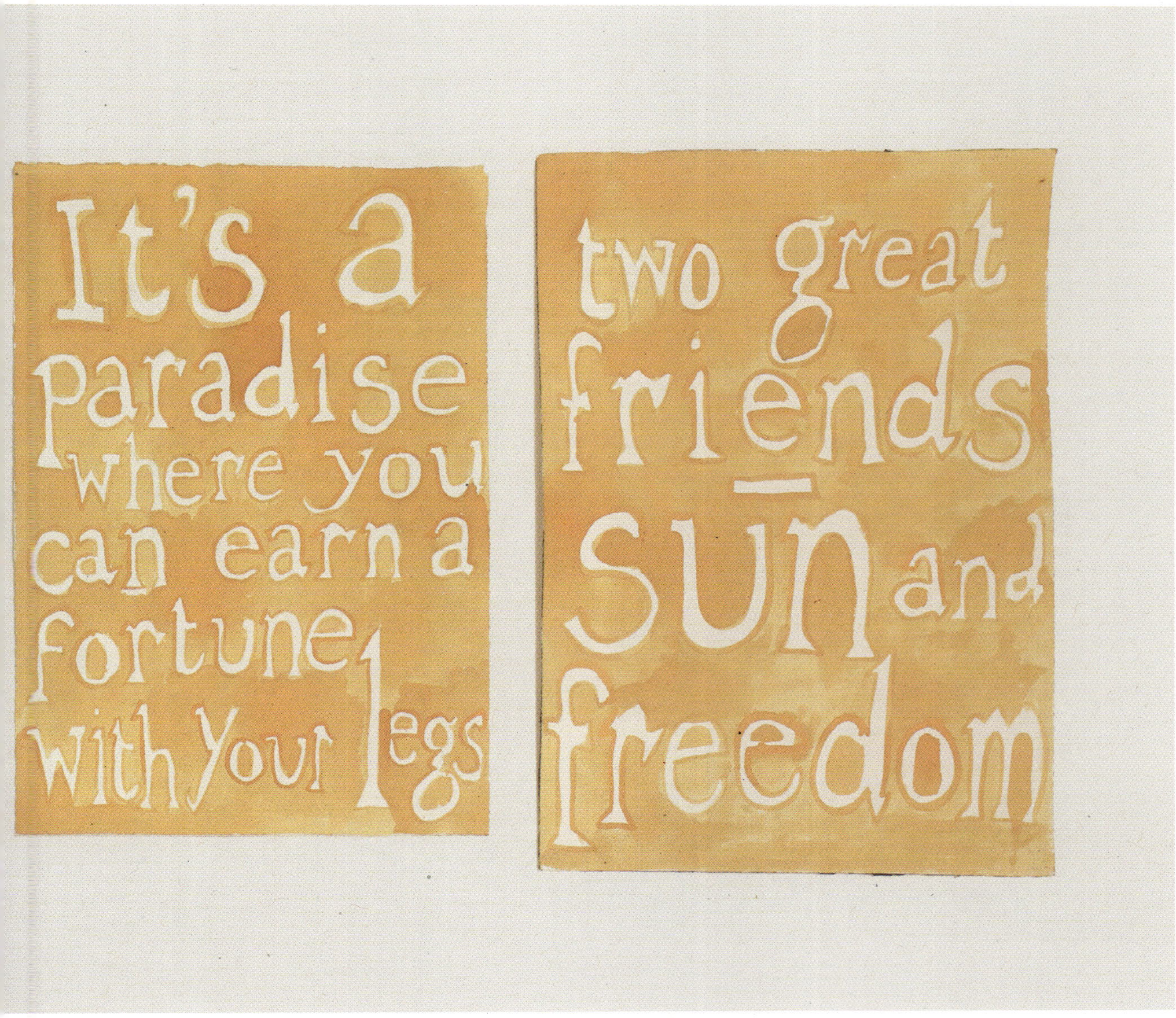
It's a paradise where you can earn a fortune with your legs
two great friends – sun and freedom

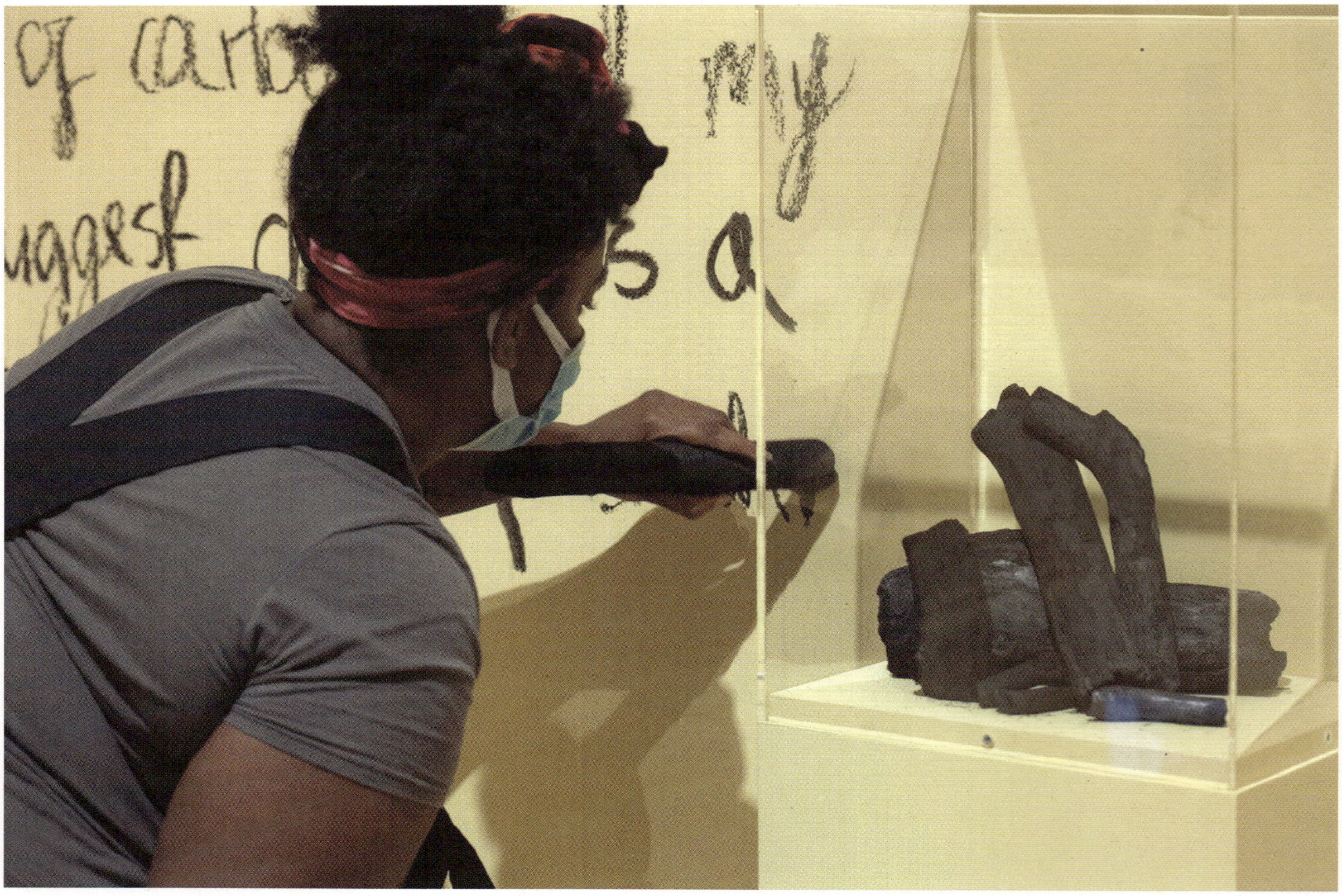

Live writing on the gallery wall by Nikita Gill of Jade Montserrat's spoken word from *Drawing Out* on the occasion of the opening of *Constellations: Care & Resistance* at Manchester Art Gallery, 12 November 2020

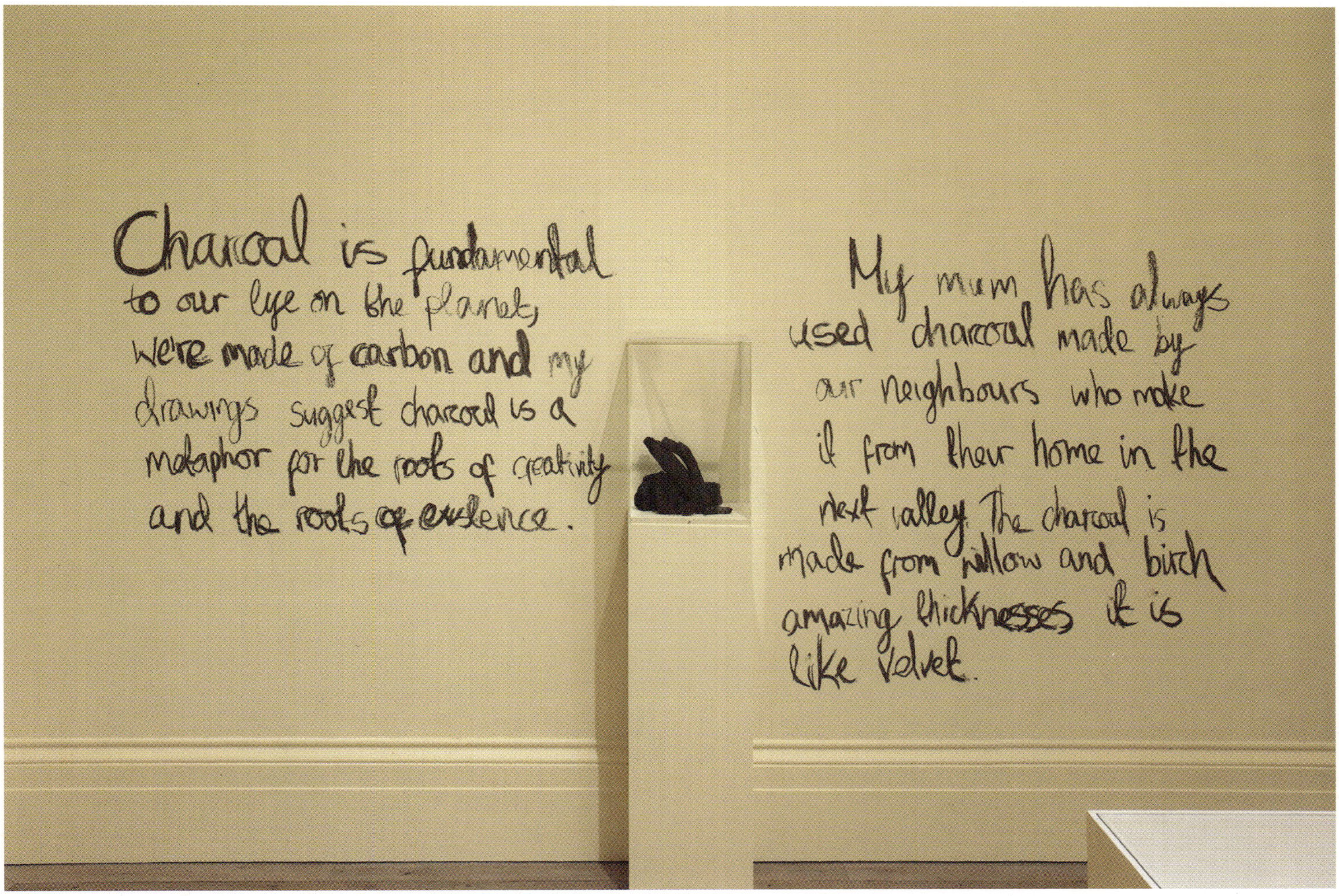

Charcoal wall drawing by Nikita Gill, part of *Drawing Out* with Jade Montserrat on the occasion of the opening of her exhibition *Constellations: Care & Resistance* at Manchester Art Gallery, 12 November 2020

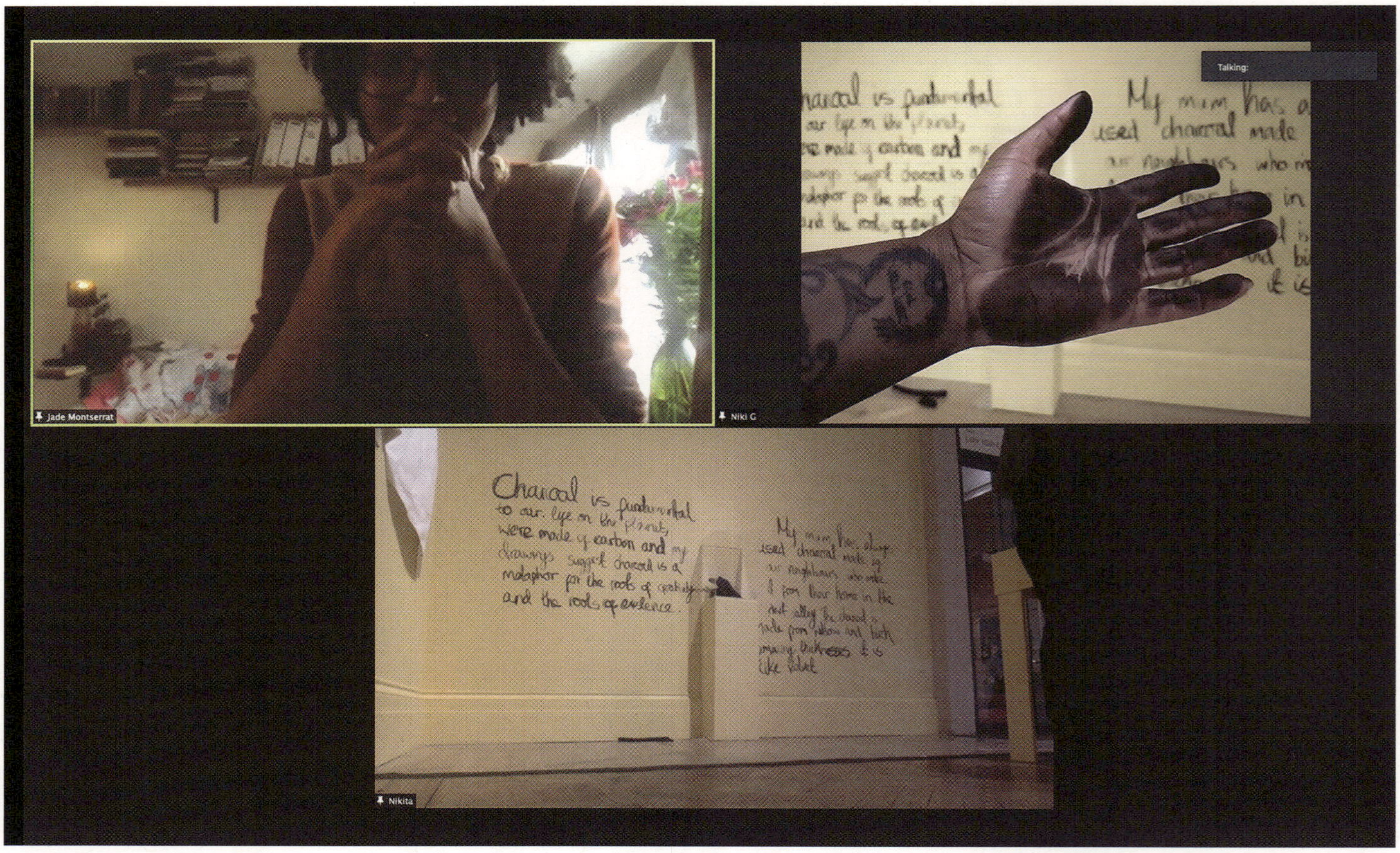

Screenshot from Jade Montserrat's *Drawing Out*, 12 November 2020

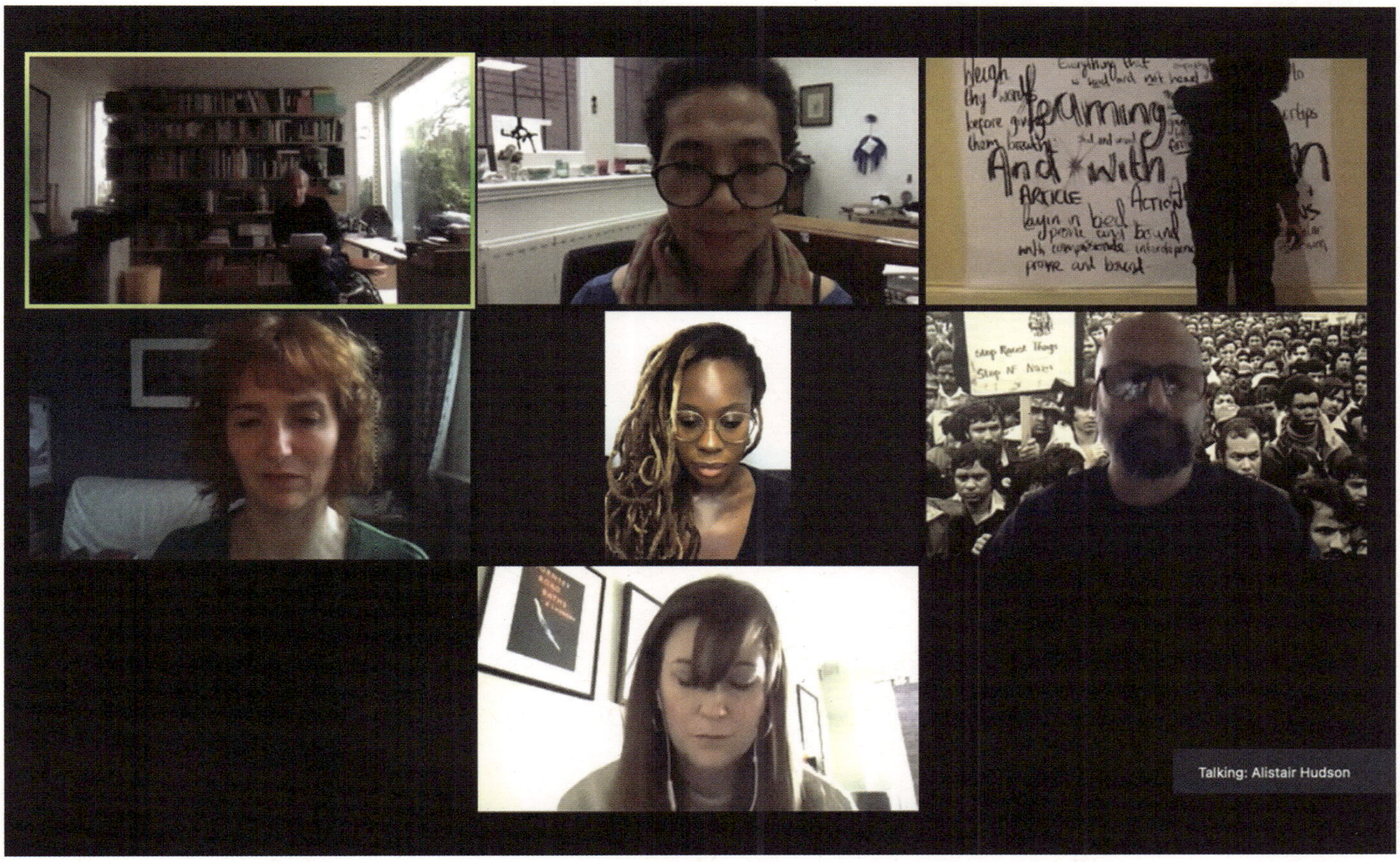

Screenshot from Jade Montserrat's online performance of *Rehearsal Methods: audition pieces for solo and collective*, 25 March 2021

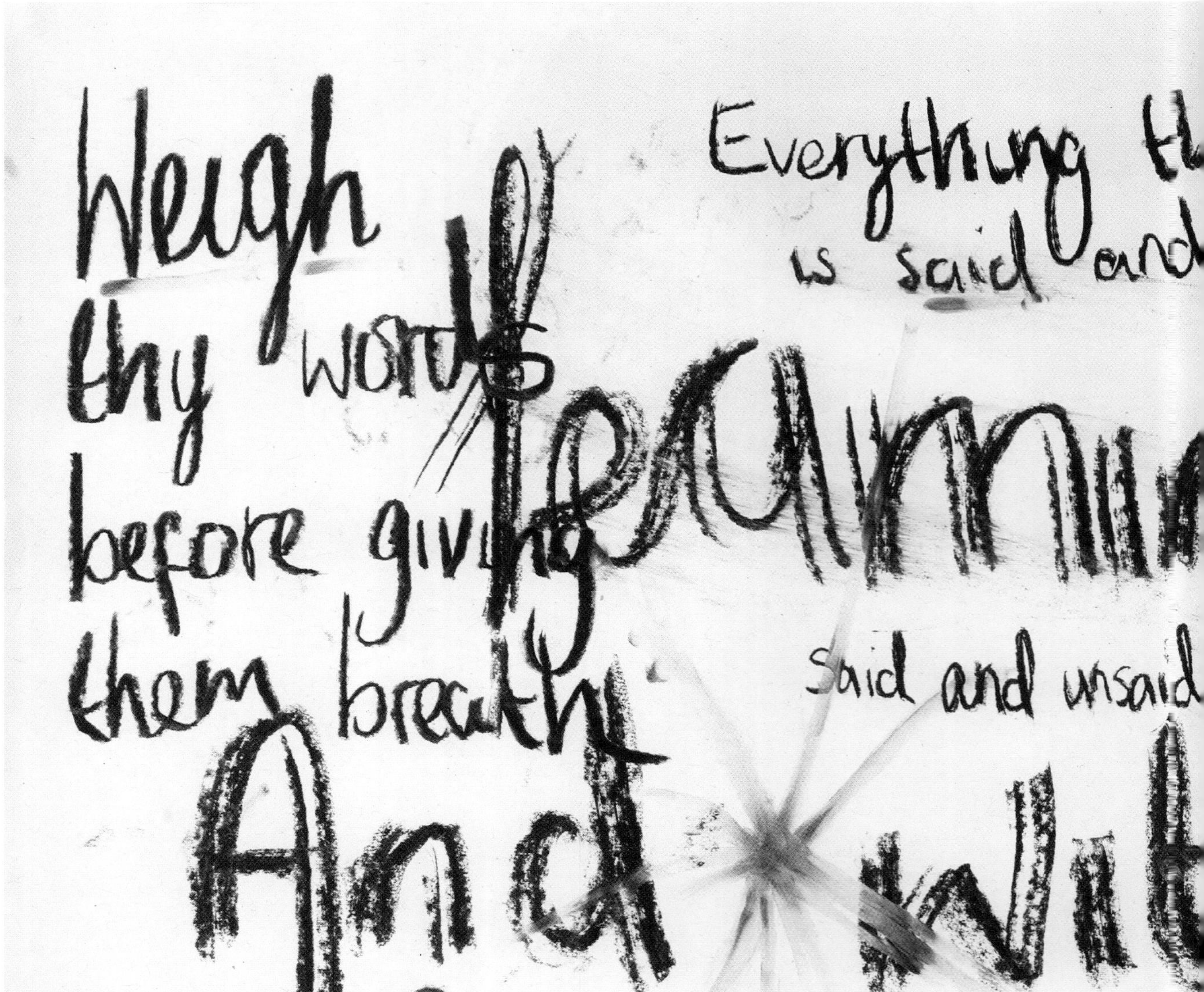

Text from Jade Montserrat's performance *Rehearsal Methods: audition pieces for solo and collective* inscribed at Manchester Art Gallery, 25 March 2021

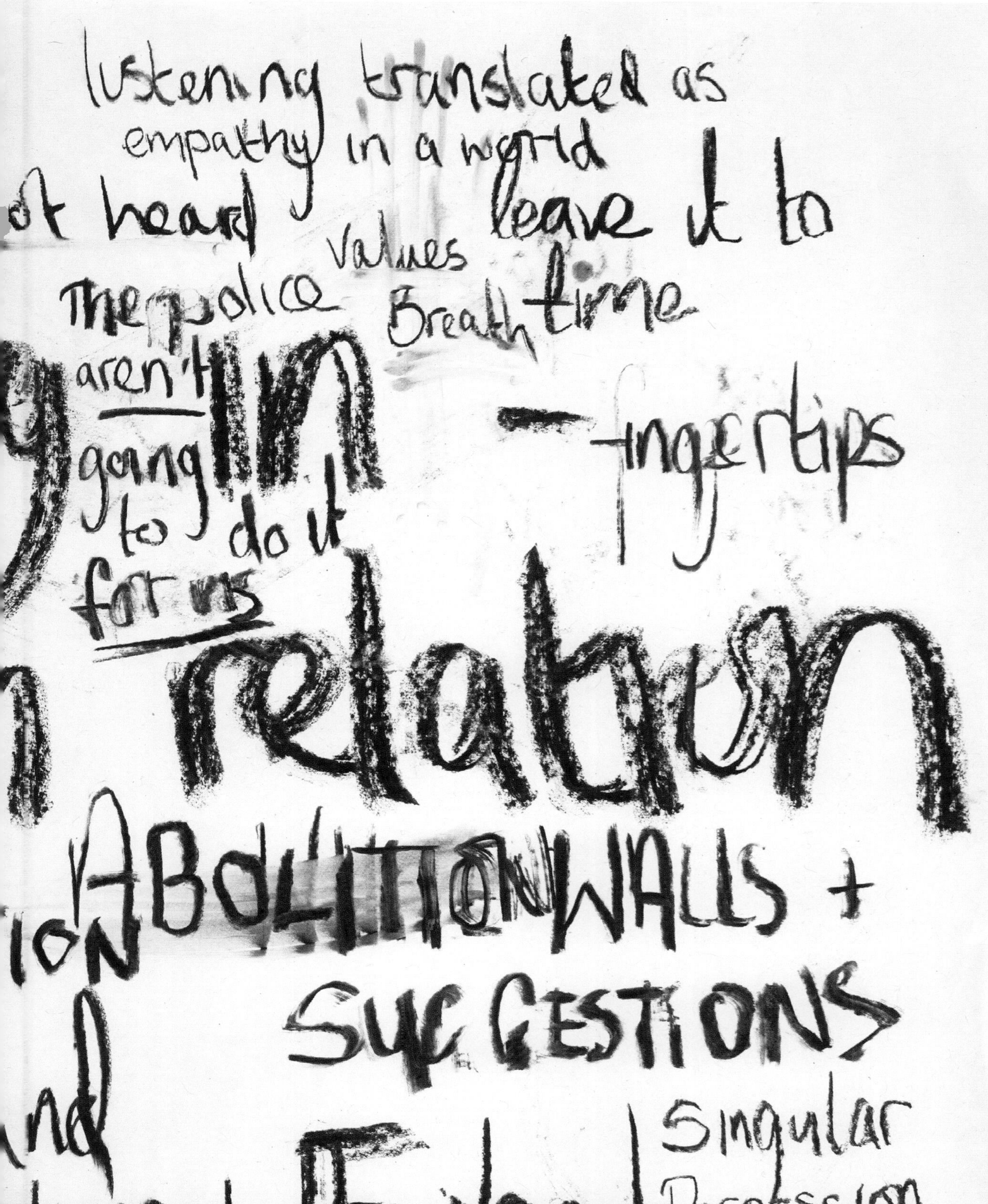
listening translated as empathy in a world
ot heard
leave it to time
Values
The police aren't going to do it for us
Breath
in
fingertips
relation
ABOLITION
WALLS + SUGGESTIONS
ION
nd
depency
Exhale
singular Possession

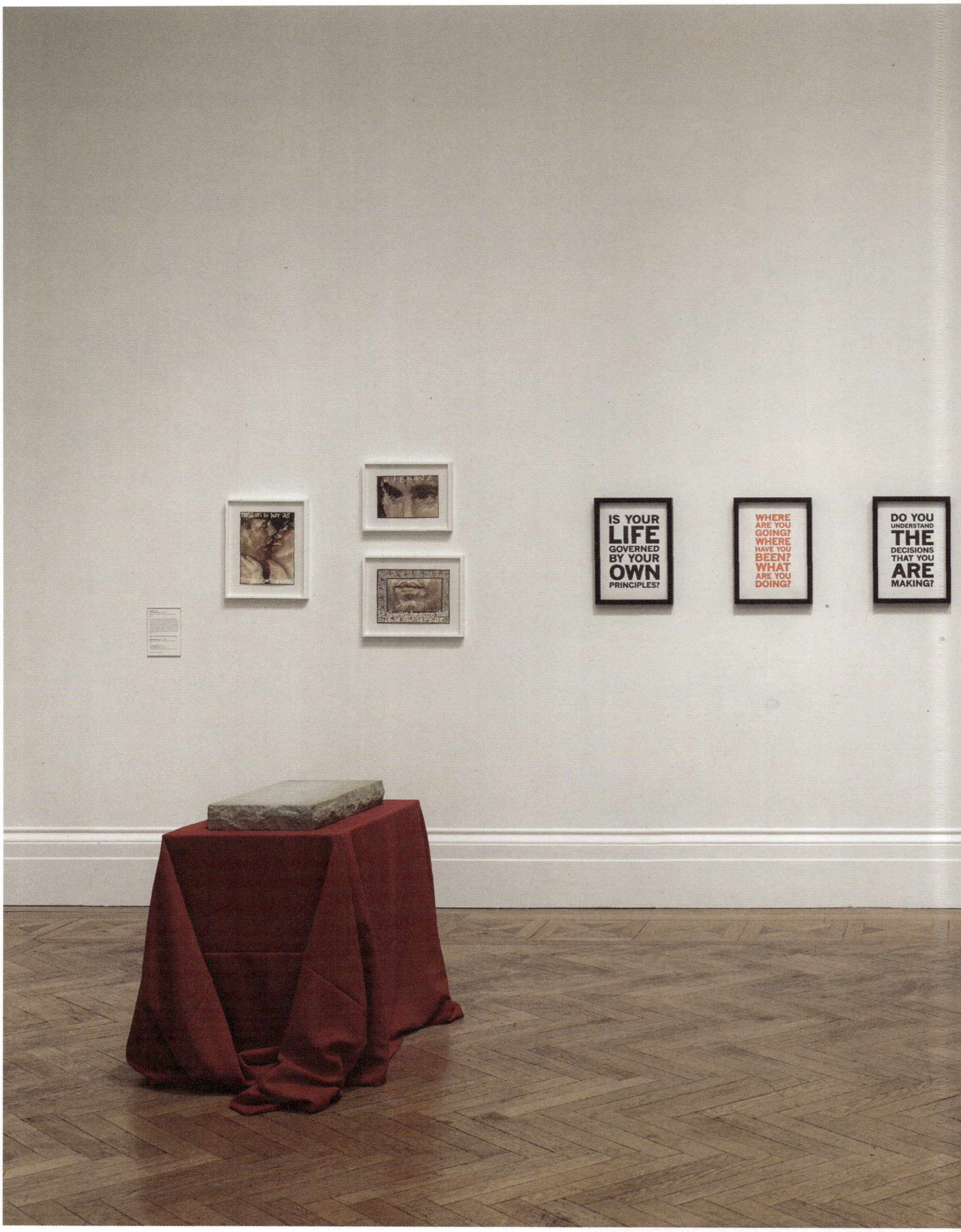

Installation view of Jade Montserrat's *Constellations: Care & Resistance*, November 2020 – October 2021 (*Shadow Revue: Ecclesiastes*, 2017, Jade Montserrat, *Some questions about us*, 2019, Mark Titchner)

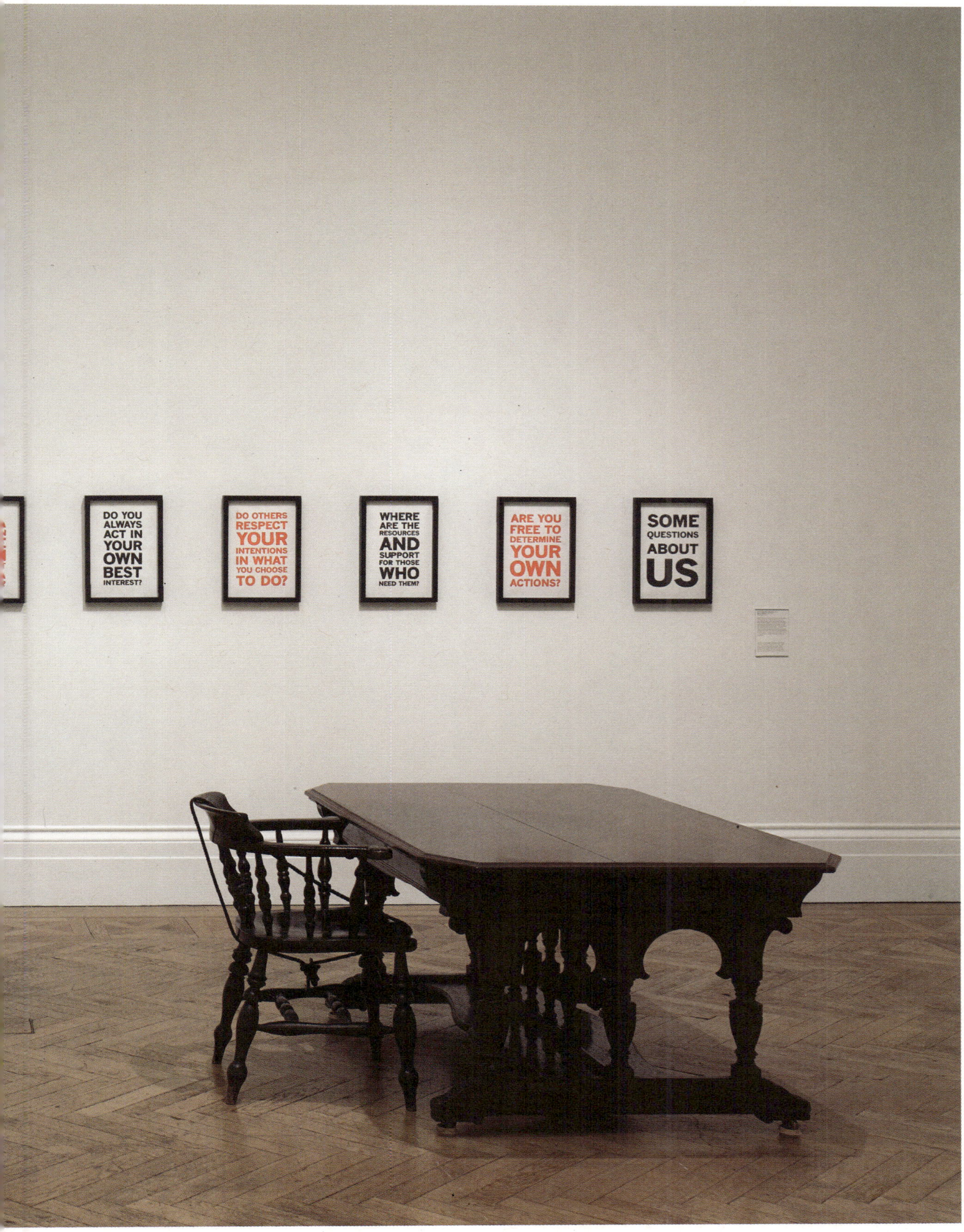
DO YOU ALWAYS ACT IN YOUR OWN BEST INTEREST?
DO OTHERS RESPECT YOUR INTENTIONS IN WHAT YOU CHOOSE TO DO?
WHERE ARE THE RESOURCES AND SUPPORT FOR THOSE WHO NEED THEM?
ARE YOU FREE TO DETERMINE YOUR OWN ACTIONS?
SOME QUESTIONS ABOUT US

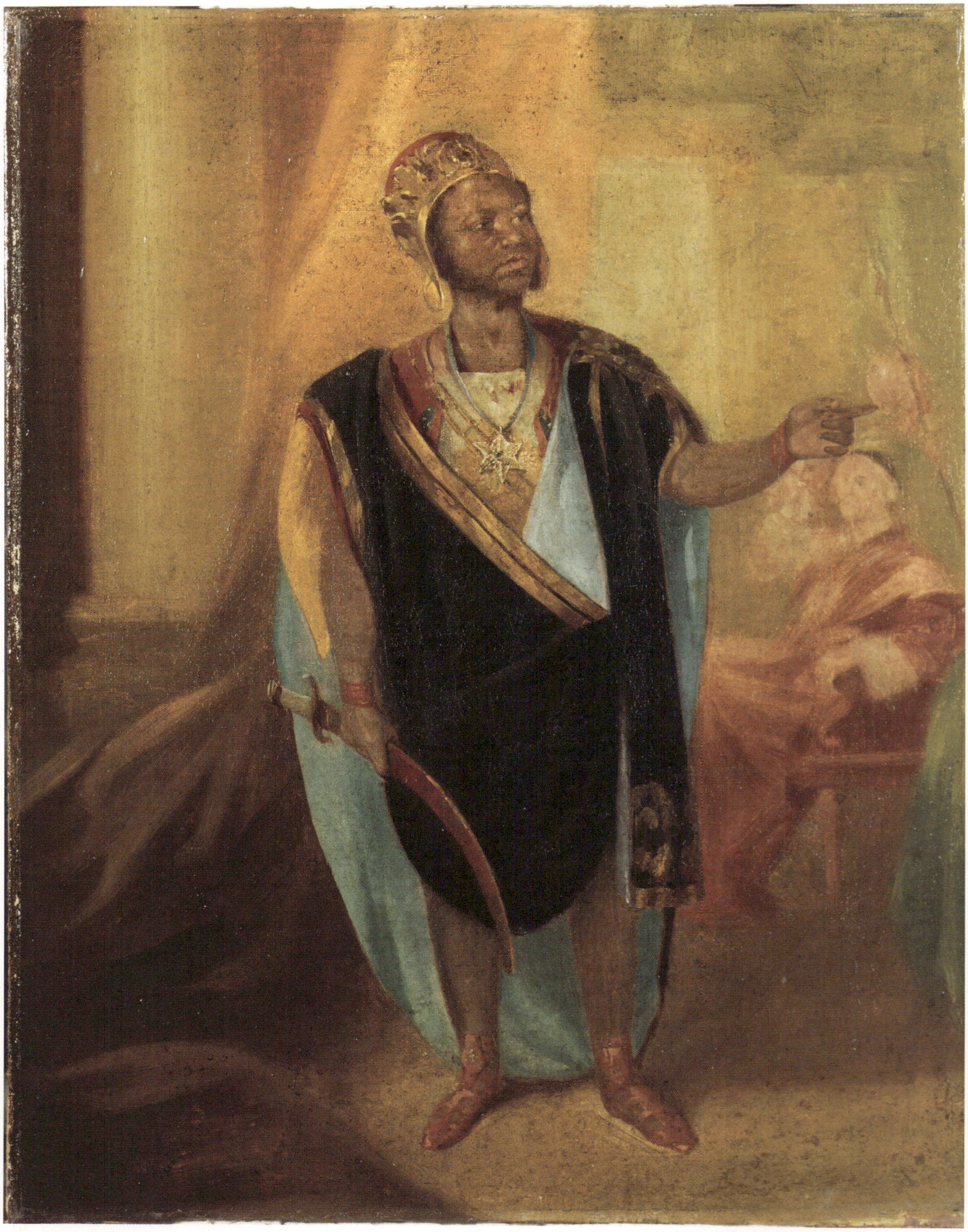

Ira Aldridge as Othello in 'Othello' by William Shakespeare, c.1848, Unkown Artist, Victoria and Albert Museum, London

ACT III

ON PUBLISHING RADICAL CONSTITUTIONS

On 27 January 2021, Jade Montserrat invited Hamja Ahsan, author of *Shy Radicals* and the Manchester-based poetry collective No Matter (Jazz Linklater, Nell Osborne, and Hilary White) to join her in the online conversation *On Publishing Radical Constitutions.* The discussion, moderated by Nikita Gill, considered the potential of a publication, what writing can do, and the notion of publishing as a political act. In this edited excerpt of the conversation, the speakers unpick the multiple meanings of the word 'constitution', discuss the history of the hunger strike as a way of rewriting boundaries and laws, the way neurodivergence undermines the neoliberal subject, and the meaning of radicalism

[Note to the reader: This conversation contains sensitive content in relation to mental health, depression, and suicide.]

NIKITA GILL

Our first question is: 'How can a publication become something we embody?'

HILARY WHITE

Taking the question of embodying a publication tangentially, I was thinking about handmaking publications, like zines and pamphlets. We've been talking about the poetry world being potentially less commodified than the art world. So much of the work in poetry gets circulated amongst friends, small publishers, small presses...

JAZZ LINKLATER

Within that, we have this confusion between the labour of doing it and the love for which you do it. Unless you have Arts Council backing, is anyone really getting paid? There are all these slippages of the place where labour starts: is it a hobby? Is it your leisure time? There's this murky area because everyone's doing stuff all the time.

HAMJA AHSAN

I question this idea of everything being quantified as labour in the first place. I'm thinking of the term 'constitution', with which this conversation is framed, and how there's a play on words in terms of how that could be used. Constitution can denote a state, or a bodily state, or a state of health. Thinking about how we embody publications, I want to insert the figure of the hunger striker here. The obvious example is Bobby Sands. Could you have a hunger striker get paid per hour? Or quantify that hunger strike in terms of the form of labour? Or does it just totally rip that whole system of quantification apart? I think this can be an interesting play on the double meaning of the word constitution. One of the things I always struggled with as an awkward, shy person was when someone asked me, 'How are you?' Imagine how the world might be different if someone instead asked, 'How is your constitution?' Going back to the hunger strike and the idea of written constitutions, Bobby Sands himself is an embodiment of texts relating back to 1916, the Easter Rising, the declaration of independence and that whole lineage of Irish literature.

What I really tried to do in *Shy Radicals*, and with *Asylum* magazine and mental health zines, is to reclaim some aspects of myself that are deemed unhealthy or unemployable. One of my favourite mental health zine collectives, The Icarus Project, reclaimed the suicidal episode as a way of totally breaking with work, school, society's pretences and standards. I'm thinking about my own depressive episodes, as someone diagnosed as a manic depressive, as a form of my body going on strike. So it's neither negative nor positive thinking, it's neither healthy nor unhealthy, but it's affirming something about my need for rest, slowing down and a limit in terms of what I can actually endure.

JADE MONTSERRAT

I wondered if the requirement for a hunger strike indicates a constitutional crisis.

HAMJA AHSAN

I think it's about rewriting the constitution through a hunger strike. I'm thinking of the Yarl's Wood hunger strikes and how they're rewriting national borders, what the human community is and what the citizen is. If you go back to Irish playwright, author and politician Terence MacSwiney, who starved to death in Brixton prison in 1920, those Irish hunger strikes were then witnessed by Ho Chi Minh and Jawaharlal Nehru, so I was always fascinated by the way an empty stomach could rock the entire British Empire. They're rewriting citizenship, rewriting dignity, and then it creates a transnational movement. In California, quite recently, you had 30,000 people on hunger strike against solitary confinement. That was directly inspired by Bobby Sands and his prison writings. You have strikes in Palestine and Guantanamo Bay. Within the Guantanamo Bay hunger strikes, you had this period with the 'War on Terror' where constitutions were effectively suspended. Constitutional rights — the right to fair trial, the writ of *habeas corpus* and the Magna Carta — were all suspended. So hunger strikes are affirmations of constitutional rights; I think they embody those pieces of writing.

There are also many forms of the human experience that aren't even written into law or constitutions. For example, my brother was in solitary confinement in a US prison for two years, and the right to human company is not in the US Bill of Rights at all. This gap was also exploited by the US against the Black Panthers generation: the Angola Three were held in solitary confinement for over 40 years. I've also felt like the discrimination and alienation I experienced as an introvert, whether that's in employment, school, the media, or decision-making, is not written into law as a constitutional right at all, so I rewrote these laws for *Shy Radicals*. I think about the case of Sophie Lancaster, who was murdered about ten years ago for being a goth. Being hated for being a goth is not recognised by a piece of legislation. Her family continues to campaign, and she has a whole cult following from rock stars because of that. It's that sort of subcultural thing, which overlaps with being recognised as an introvert. It has no form of legal protection, but maybe in the world to come we will write constitutions for goths.

JADE MONTSERRAT

That's not an unfamiliar story, living in Whitby: the number of suicides of people who are seen as different here floors one, really...

NIKITA GILL

There's another comment I wanted to read out here: 'I'm interested in the modest approach as activism and how language can be modest but equally confrontational.'

HAMJA AHSAN

Part of the practice of *Shy Radicals* is also inventing political gestures towards 'shy power'. I'm interested in how things such as staring into space, staring at the floor, or depressive passivity are also embodiments of contentment or discontentment. I'm thinking of Ho Chi Minh staring at a lake, or Rosa Parks sitting on a bus. The entire book is a detour exploration of that form of activism. One of my great heroes is the human rights lawyer Gareth Peirce, who represented everyone from the Guildford Four to the Hillsborough families, the striking miners, and she also represented my brother. She's an embodiment of fighting against the oppressive aspects of the British state, but she has a particular manner of speaking, which is a bit like a mouse.

JAZZ LINKLATER

I also think the act of publishing and organising is a very modest form of political action, especially in these DIY and collaborative communities that we're working in. As No Matter, we use our time to platform other people: we're trying to find a way to quietly give them the space to be heard and also the money to be able to practice. I'm thinking about how the 'behind the scenes' work is a kind of modest and quiet activism. It's necessary for somebody to be doing it all the time, so that the louder politics can be heard.

HAMJA AHSAN

We also have the example of former British Prime Minister Clement Attlee introducing the NHS and the welfare state. He was a really quiet, shy person who used to sit awkwardly and write poems in the corner of meetings with tubthumping trade unionists. You look at his portrait in the National Portrait Gallery in London, and he looks like a bank clerk. This was in the age of the 'charismatic fascist' (like Mussolini) and yet he won two general elections against Churchill and introduced probably the most socialist policies we've had, and that is quite a strengthening thing. Also Patrick Pearse, who was the leader of the Easter Rising in Ireland, opened a school for sensitive boys in Dublin where he'd teach Celtic poetry and languages. It was for boys with a sensitive disposition and simultaneously a radical, decolonial school. It's still a national monument in Ireland. There's also this organisation called Gentle Radical in Cardiff, which embodies many of these processes.

NIKITA GILL

The next question I'd like to ask the speakers is: if we invoke the constitutional crisis, can it be approached as an apparatus for transformation? What I mean by a 'constitutional crisis' is how political governance ignores the needs of the people or ignores the needs of the body and personal governance.

JAZZ LINKLATER

We've touched on this play on the word 'constitution' and its multiple meanings. So what is a constitution? It's the way something is constituted. That means that it can be broken down into its constituent parts, and once you've broken it down, it can be reconstituted. You can take various parts of it and maybe reconfigure them towards a different end, towards the transformation of something. All the work we're talking about here is collaborative by necessity, and maybe everything is necessarily collaborative to a certain degree. So, can you separate the legislative constitution that we're talking about from the healthy body and one's personal constitution? Of course you can separate them, but only as a conceptual distinction. What's the use of making that conceptual distinction? Who has the power to do it? Who is able to say where bodies start and end and how they integrate with other bodies, which might include systems of legislation?

I've been thinking a lot about how in Anne Boyer's 2019 book *The Undying*, she talks about how the neoliberal narrative of sickness, especially cancer, is put on the individual. When you're diagnosed with cancer, your body will be subjected to all of these different measurements, remeasurements and tests. They weigh all of this up and give you all this data, but no one's ever going to go to where you live and measure the air quality of your neighbourhood, or measure what's in your drinking water. So then, you have these two constitutions: on one level, it's the system of healthcare which is legislating the boundary of the personal constitution, the individual body. The healthcare system is narrativising the boundary of the body and it's saying: 'As a portable being, we can put you in this machine and give you an MRI scan, but the air you breathe in and out is not part of your body.' But, obviously, if you look at it from another angle, air is clearly a very integral part of the body.

NELL OSBORNE

This is fundamental to the neurodiversity and disability movement in general, isn't it Hamja? This idea that we understand our environments in relation to structural forces, as things that we need to change rather than our behaviour.

HAMJA AHSAN

The word 'constituent' just came up and I'm thinking about how it feels so inadequate or soulless in the sense of Members of Parliament and their constituencies. Connecting to what's just been said, only people with certain personality types can run for MP. I don't think people like me and you could ever actually run for election. So the extrovert neurotypical person gets to represent us, but we can't represent them. The entire process of decision-making in the adversarial parliamentary chamber, with all its simultaneous noise, creates an environment in which most people can't function.

In contrast, there's a feminist performance artist called Lois Weaver who invented this public address system called *The Long Table*, in which people come together around a dinner table to talk in a very improvised way, with a very limited series of rules, with no conclusion to begin or to end. This has also been adapted for the neurodiversity movement by the artist Daniel Oliver. He included elements to block out noise and centre the discourse of guests around neurodiversity. What if you could take that *Long Table* format out of experimental theatre and integrate it into everyday life, like having a coffee, or going to the pub? What if we didn't have select committees or debates, and that was actually the way in which our political representatives drafted things? When you have these Long Tables, you can just draw and doodle on the table, so you share your idle or informal thoughts. If this sort of non-formalised, non-technocratic language could be part of all the spaces in between the law, how would the world be different?

I'm also interested in connecting to the point you made earlier, Nell, about being diagnosed quite recently with autism. Has it become a different type of subject now you have a point of identification and diagnosis?

NELL OSBORNE

Yes, I like to think about things and I find it very empowering to have this framework to think through, which isn't as gendered — not so dysphoric, more neutral, I guess. It's allowed me to think about the way that autistic people are bad neoliberal subjects, which I think is really cool. This is the work that I want to be doing now, thinking through disability: it seeds loads of different kinds of ideas, like how autism is racialised and it's ableist. I used to have feminism as my main lens and I'm still interested in feminism, but this has shifted my perspective dramatically.

HILARY WHITE

I like this idea of being a bad subject, part of this kind of refusalist position.

JADE MONTSERRAT

There's a question from audience member Joy here. I wonder whether you'd like to ask it directly?

JOY

I'm neurodiverse, so the way my brain works means I can say it better than I could write it. I've been thinking a lot about language, and somebody recently told me that the English language is a law-based language, so it's confined within that. Language, to me, tries to point to something finite, or to a complete understanding of one thing because we have a word for it. So I'm interested in how language and constitutions can be radical and freeing, if their roots have been damaging to people. Because sometimes you can't explain a body, or a body doesn't feel explained through a language, or an experience can't be explained through language. When language can be so static, how does it free those who are still morphing?

JADE MONTSERRAT

I think we'll take your question with us as we're making our publication. It makes me think of Audre Lorde's writing, but it also brings me back to Rivca Rubin, who was in the conversation for Act I. Rivca was talking about 'putting words in the bin' and I think that triggered me to suddenly feel like I wanted to own all the words so I could reclaim and reshape them. But that depends on how you're going to use them, and who is going to use them. That's the dilemma, isn't it? The words aren't free as long as they're abused, and by abused I mean that they can directly harm somebody else.

HAMJA AHSAN

Part of my practice as an artist, writer and curator has always involved inventing my own neologisms, from 'extrovert supremacy' to 'Islamic-extremely-nice-ism', from 'developmentia' (which is a cross between development and dementia) to 'beaurocrotics' (which is a cross between bureaucracy and neurotics). Those are ways I've created forms or vocabularies of resistance. Words can adapt and travel somewhere else — like 'boycott', which comes out of the Irish struggle.[1]

But then during the Bush era of the War on Terror, there were all sorts of reinventions of oppressive language like 'extraordinary rendition' (meaning kidnapping

[1] The word 'boycott' comes from the name of Captain Charles Boycott, who was the agent of an absentee landlord in Ireland. The tactic of 'boycotting' was successfully used against him by the Irish Land League in 1880.

and torturing someone) or 'waterboarding' (which simulated someone drowning to death). There was a whole new poetics of abuse, a form of rewriting language.

NIKITA GILL

We have another question here: 'I noticed that the word 'radical' was used quite a lot. And I would like to know how each one of you conceptualises it, and in what way you use it. It's a linguistic question, a question of etymology and the meaning that comes with it. Also, with this in mind, there are certain buzzwords that like to appear in contemporary art discourses. I'm wondering about your personal definitions of 'radical'?'

JADE MONTSERRAT

I wonder if I sometimes use it as a provocation, but I think when I use that word I actually mean 'overhaul'.

HAMJA AHSAN

For me, it means seeing things clearly, paying attention. Seeing things as embodiments of power, rather than necessary structures. In Britain, and also internationally, there's quite a disturbing way in which the term 'radical' has been adopted by mainstream media. The meaning of radicalisation and deradicalisation have been set by the security state and the Home Office. There are technocratic systems everywhere, like NGOs, law courts, or even the bureaucratic welfare state, but radicalism is the actual pulse and lifeblood of things. There's this poem that Bobby Sands wrote in prison, about this sort of refusal that goes through time. I think of it as this larger, almost cosmological thing, like a river running through things, or a spark or flame.

JAZZ LINKLATER

I really treasure some of those contradictions within the term 'radical', like Hamja was just saying, as with the state's use of the term 'radicalisation'. But they all do the same thing, because it's about the extreme. It means inherently extreme, or inherently, *utterly* something.

NELL OSBORNE

The danger of the proliferation of the word radical is when it becomes an aesthetic, and I think it always needs to be a contextual dynamic. It means refusing to perform within a particular system, so it's always tied to the system. I think experimental poetry is very prone to calling things radical and using really radical theories in quite metaphorical ways, so they very quickly become *not* radical.

HAMJA AHSAN

There's also the way that radical is used as a term for the right — such as the EDL (English Defence League), or Donald Trump, or whatever — but I don't consider those radical because they're just reflections of the centre: embodiments of the *Daily Mail*, aspects of government policy, or keeping borders. The way it's used in the British mainstream is to refer to everything that deviates from the liberal centre, which isn't an adequate constitutional system.

JAZZ LINKLATER

In many different contexts, radical means 'root', doesn't it? So in linguistics and maths it's the root of the word or number, and in music you talk about the radical of a chord. There's the idea of the rhizome, and lateral connectivity in non-hierarchical ways. So, what is radical? Is it being in direct opposition to hierarchies of power? That's the way that we're connecting with each other, through these sideways movements.

JADE MONTSERRAT

I just wanted to read aloud this paragraph that's been quoted here from Fred Moten's 2018 book *Stolen Life*:

> Blackness is enthusiastic social vision, given in (non)performance, as the surrealization of space and time, the inseparability of gravity and matter, fabric's fabrication, field's feel, rub's rub, plain's chant, an endlessly ante-inaugural endlessness of means, an empillowed, haptically ham-boned coinstrumentality of care, in caressive sound and anachoreographic sounding. Anticipating originary correction with self-defensive division and (re)collection, it goes way back, long before the violent norm, as an impure informality to come. Its open and initiatory counterpleasures reveal the internal, public resource of our common sense/s, where flavorful touch is all bound up with falling into the general antagonistic embrace. That autonomous song and dance is our intellectual descent; it neither opposes nor follows from dissent but, rather, gives it a chance. Consent to that submergence is terrible and beautiful. Moreover, the apparent (racial) exclusivity of the (under)privilege of claiming this dis/ability serially impairs — though it can never foreclose - the discovery that the priority of sovereign regulation is false. In order to get the plain sense of this, you have to use your imagination.

'Blackness is enthusiastic social vision' — that's so good!

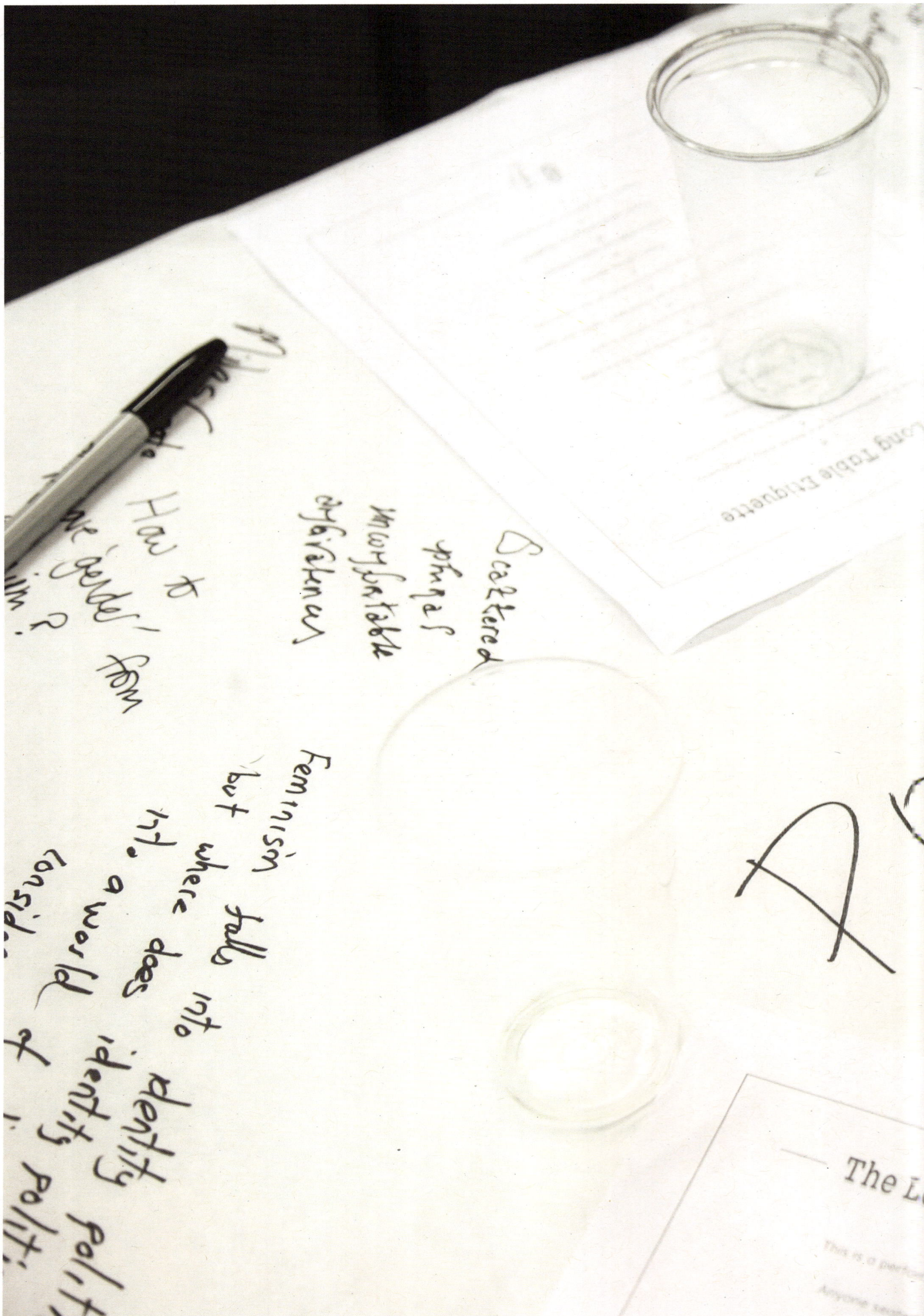

The Long Table on Live Art and Feminism with Lois Weaver, 2013. Live Art Development Agency, *Restock, Rethink, Reflect Three: on Live Art and Feminism.* Image: Alex Eisenberg.

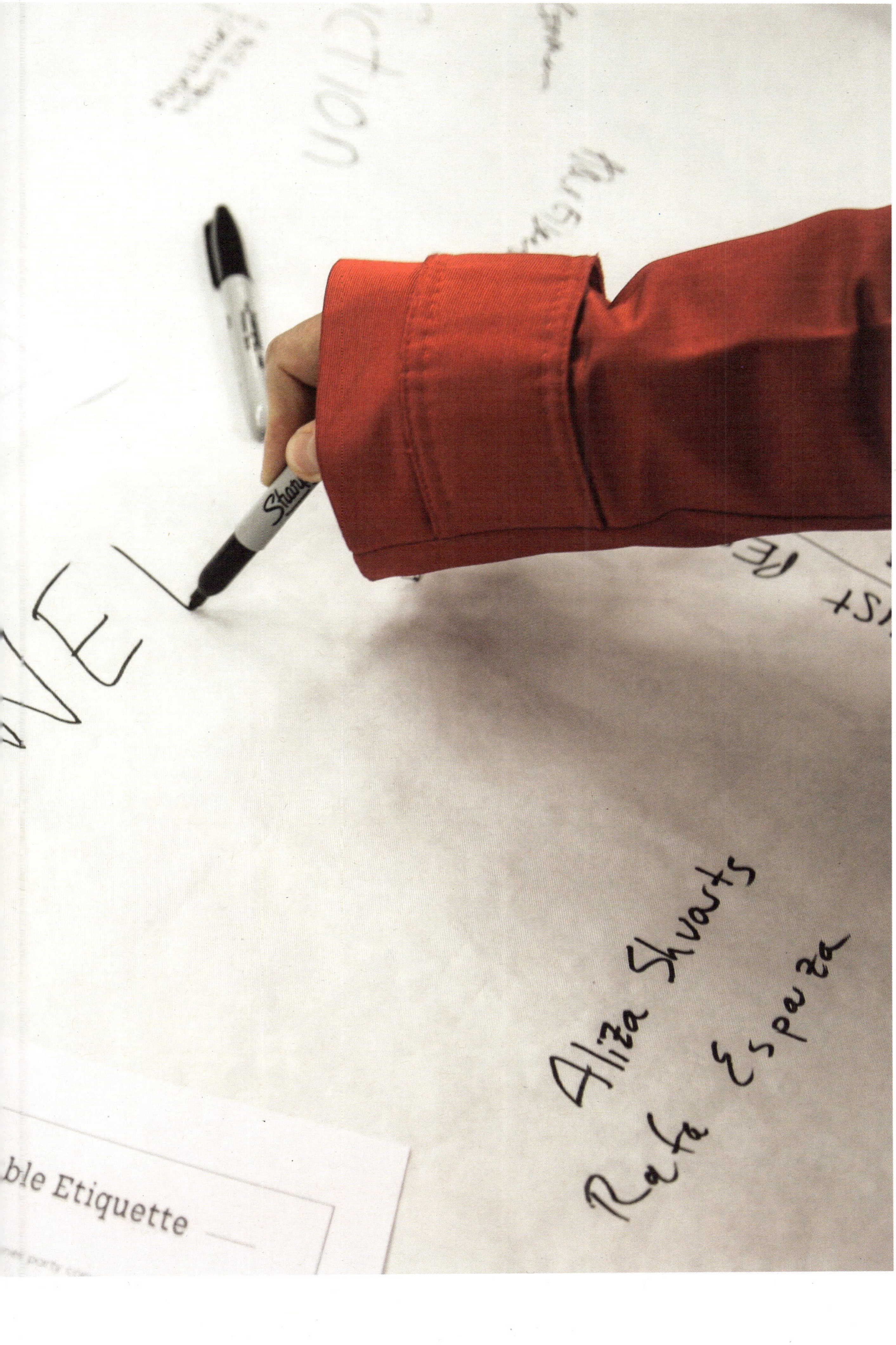
Aliza Shvarts
Rafa Esparza
ble Etiquette

The Long Table Etiquette

This is a performance of a dinner table conversation

Anyone seated at the table is a guest performer

Talk is the only course

No one will moderate

But a host may assist you

It is a democracy

To participate, simply take an empty seat at the table

If the table is full you can request a seat

If you leave the table you can come back again and again

Feel free to write your comments on the tablecloth

There can be silence

There might be awkwardness

There could always be laughter

There is an end, but no conclusion.

Long Table Protocol created by Lois Weaver

Coming To The Table

The Long Table is a format for discussion that uses the setting of a domestic dinner table as a means to generate public conversation. Conceived in 2003 by Lois Weaver in response to the divided nature of conventional panel discussions, the Long Table allows voices to be heard equally, disrupting hierarchical notions of 'expertise.' It was inspired by Maureen Gorris's film *Antonia's Line*, the central image of which is a dinner table getting longer and longer to accommodate a growing family of outsiders, eccentrics and friends – until finally it has to be moved outside. Since then, the Table has been set at institutions and festivals worldwide, and invited hundreds of people to sit and share their views on myriad topics. The Long Table is an open-source format; you are welcome to use it as a means of generating discussion on any subject you choose.

• •

Setting The Table

A space, light focused on the Table, microphones

The Long Table is also a performance; people can participate by sitting at the Table, in the light, and using microphones, spectate by watching and listening from the outside, and move between these roles as and when they choose.

A long table, twelve chairs

Approximately two banqueting tables in length: any longer, or with any more participants, and you will struggle to maintain a single conversation.

Surrounding chairs for spectators

Well-spaced and easily accessible, to allow for the free-flowing choreography of coming and going from the Table.

White tablecloth, marker pens

Everyone at the Table can write their own comments and notes, to help document the conversation. The cloth provides a physical record of the event.

A hostess, and etiquette

The Table will moderate itself, and there is no need for anyone to 'tie up loose ends' at the end; however, a hostess can ensure everyone follows the etiquette, and close the conversation at the set time.

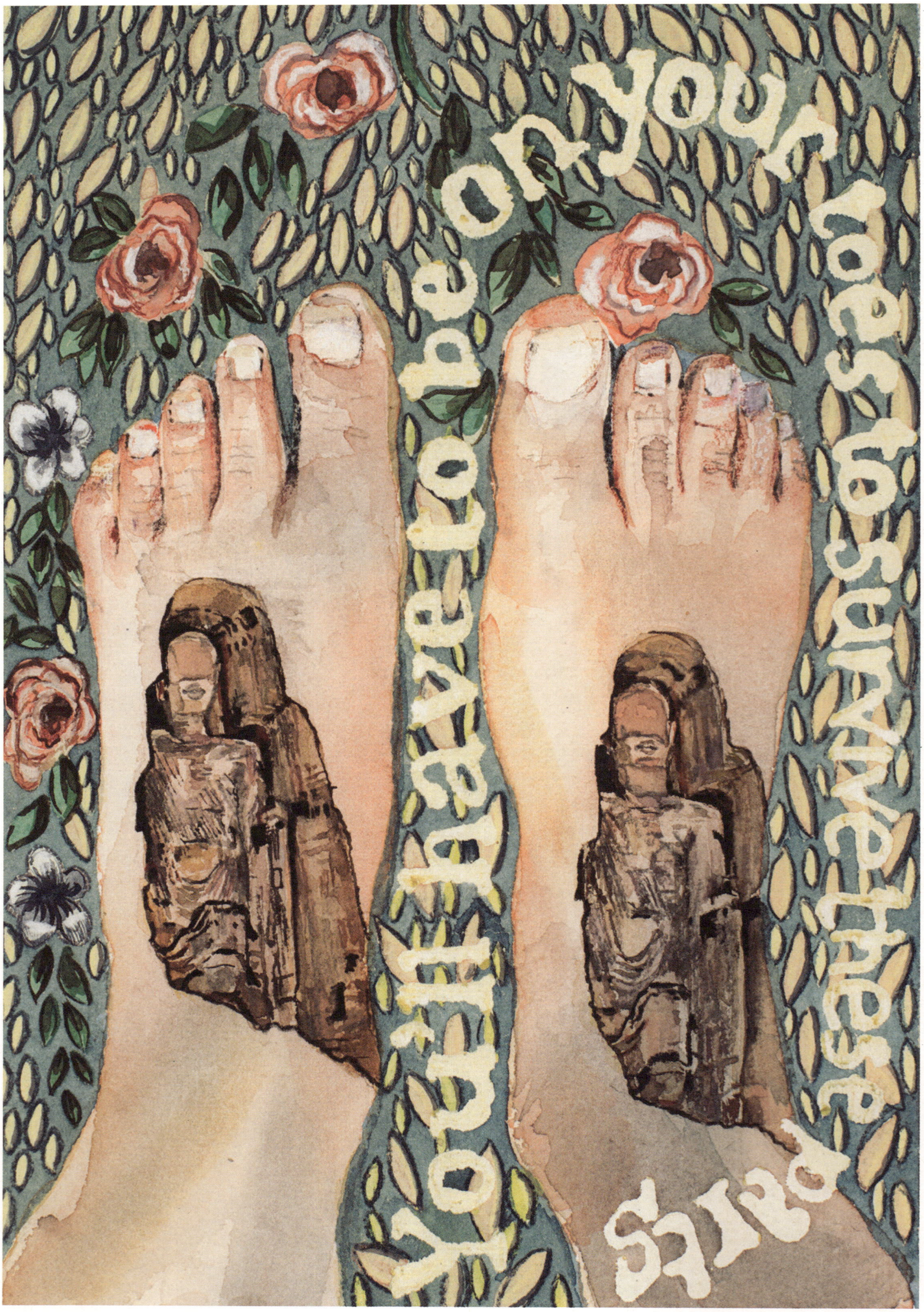

You'll have to be on your toes to survive these parts, 2017

EXPLORING BLACK ATLANTIC LIVES IN THE NORTH OF ENGLAND WITH JADE MONTSERRAT

ALAN RICE

...globalisation must never be read as a simple process of cultural homogenisation; it is always an articulation of the local, of the specific and the global. Therefore, there will always be specificities — of voices, of positioning, of identity, of cultural traditions, of histories, and these are the conditions of enunciation which allow us to speak. We speak with distinctive voices; but we speak with the logic of a cultural-global, which opens a conversation between us, which would not have been possible otherwise.[1]

Stuart Hall's description of globalisation's contingency on the local and the specific is key to understanding the way African diasporan artists, such as Jade Montserrat, make art in relation to their very local Britishness. This is too often lost in discussions of metropolitan artists with their transnational valences. Montserrat is well-positioned for the *Future Collect* programme in Manchester due to her insistence on locality in her artwork, which makes her able to perfectly realise a dynamic and situated mode for interacting with the collections at the Gallery.

Stuart Hall's invocation of 'the local, the specific and the global' is exemplified in Montserrat's interest in James Northcote's 1826 portrait of the famous American-born actor Ira Aldridge (1807-67). Showing Aldridge in character as Othello, the portrait is a key work to interrogate through Montserrat's artistic reflections. Montserrat explains how the experience of using the career of transnational performer and activist Josephine Baker in her earlier work to discuss cosmopolitanism and localism is replicated in this later work. As she explained herself:

I wanted to interrogate issues around Manchester as 'Cottonopolis', and the significance of the solidarity between mill workers and slaves during the cotton famine in the 1860s. Like in my earlier work on Josephine Baker, I'm catching up with the histories and understanding the amnesias and the erasures, and then trying to focus in on individuals who changed the landscape. Josephine Baker opens up the possibility of being at once European and cosmopolitan, and how racism works here in contrast to America. And equally, Ira Aldridge opens up these horizons for me to think about not just my position, but how the regions function to either obfuscate or help create a legacy.[2]

Ira Aldridge is almost a case study in how the regions were able to help create a legacy for a Black performer, in contrast to the harsh environment of London. Aldridge had arrived in Britain in 1825 as a virtual fugitive from New York and its vicious racism. From 1821, Aldridge had been involved in William Alexander Brown's African Grove and African Theatre in New York, which had been subject to virulent racist attacks in the press and physical riots in 1822, eventually being forced to close in 1824. Unfortunately, the racism followed him across the Atlantic. In a particularly vicious review, *The Times* reacted against a man of African descent playing Shakespeare in the following terms: 'Owing to the shape of his lips, it is utterly impossible for him to pronounce English in such a manner as to satisfy even the unfastidious ears of the gallery.'[3] Meanwhile, in Manchester, a dynamic, humanistic portrait of Aldridge as the first Black man to play Othello on the English stage was being produced, which gave lie to the racist description of him in the London press. There was also a press rebuttal, particularly in the *Manchester Gazette's* review of Aldridge's final performance at the Theatre Royal in the city. The review had an abolitionist slant, discussing how, 'He performed

[1] Hall, S. *Critical Dialogues in Cultural Studies*, Routledge, 1996, p. 407.
[2] Montserrat, J. *Future Collect Study Day:Jade Montserrat in Conversation with Alan Rice*, iniva, 27 May 2021.
[3] *The Times*, 11 October 1825, p. 2.

in a manner which practically contradicts the argument of the advocates of slavery, that the sable race are deficient in intellect.'[4] As Theresa Saxon discusses in her pioneering article on Aldridge in Manchester, Liverpool and Lancaster:

> Whereas, in London the body of the black performer was arrogated in the service of pro-slavery racist rhetoric, in Manchester Aldridge was discussed as a performer of skill and intellect, and thus as a body of evidence to prove all that was wrong with slavery.[5]

To an extent, the reception of Aldridge's performances in the north and the making of such a sympathetic portrait worked against the invisibility that the experience of the imperial capital had brought upon him. In this imperial narrative, Black people in Britain didn't have the right to take on the words of the Bard. In a sense, Aldridge's whole career was around asserting that he *did* have that right, and not only in Britain. He travelled to Poland, Russia, Hungary, and all over Europe performing in prestigious theatres, showing that he had the right as a human being, and as someone who'd lived in Britain and who spoke the English language, had as much the right as everyone else to speak those words. In fact, he performed Shakespeare as the only actor speaking in the English tongue, as the rest of the text was spoken in Polish, Russian, and Hungarian. Maybe this was his ultimate revenge on the racists, being the interlocutor of the Bard's tongue to the foreign ear.

So, there's a way of moving, in a sense, from invisibility to visibility through Shakespeare. Aldridge says, 'Yes, I have the right.' In Europe, he even played King Lear in white face. This is an incredible reversal, a means of thinking about a kind of hypervisibility, which draws attention to his status as a Black man playing a white man. Far from being meek in the presence of the great playwright and his reputation, Aldridge's performative brilliance is to claim his right to take to the stage. American-born and by 1863 so assimilated to Shakespearean mores as to become a British citizen. In another twist, Aldridge's sojourns in northern England also took him to Montserrat's hometown:

> And then, of course, since I've learned that Ira Aldridge came to my hometown, Scarborough, twice, and his son died there, which is just a whole other turn up. And I suppose what it sparked is– the depths will come later I'm sure, but the surface for me is that this is really important knowledge around, again, representation. I think there are what seem to be uphill struggles locally, or how we're seeing nationally as well, following on from last year's [social media posts of] black squares by organisations who are in solidarity [with the Black Lives Matter protests] — but how that solidarity is implemented remains open, still. I think that what it does is it makes me more determined to learn more about Ira, and to carry that awareness of this important figure in our history forward together. It's knowledge that I hope becomes received more widely. And also, I was just thinking about Ingrid Pollard's work and about reclamation of landscape itself and the countryside. What knowing about Ira Aldridge here does is reaffirm that reclamation as well, in a way, for me personally.[6]

Montserrat's invocation of Ingrid Pollard here relates to the 1988 work *Pastoral*

[4] *Manchester Gazette*, 24 February 1827, p.3.
[5] Saxon, T. 'Ira Aldridge in the North of England; Provincial Theatre and the Politics of Abolition', *Britain's Black Past*, Gerzina, G. (ed.), Liverpool University Press, 2020, pp.275-93, p.287.
[6] Montserrat, J. Future Collect Study Day: Jade Montserrat in Conversation with Alan Rice, iniva, 27 May 2021.

Interlude. In this the artist portrays a Black walker taking a rest with a camera on her knees, and delineates how the Black experience is only usually imagined within an urban environment. 'I thought I liked the Lake District when I wandered lonely as a Black face in a sea of white. A visit to the countryside is always accompanied by a feeling of unease, dread.'[7] This disjuncture is important to Montserrat, too. Interrogating those landscapes that are meant to be alien for Black people, making them hers, belonging in that space, is crucial to much of her work.

The politics of this becomes more vital in increasingly polarised times. An academic report commissioned by the National Trust on the links between its properties, historic slavery and colonialism, first released in interim form in September 2020,[8] became a weapon in a cultural war unleashed by the UK government against its findings. Montserrat has commented directly on the way this row impacts on the vital issue of disseminating Black history more widely. Montserrat spoke to me about hearing a discussion with the author of the report, Professor Corinne Fowler, on Radio 4, and how that highlighted the historical problematics of Black presence that the report was trying to address.

> And I really recognised that, from personal experience around being a 'problem in the landscape', the problematics around it. And what was surprising was, when the interviewer, the journalist, was discussing country houses' histories as linked to the slave trade as 'alleged'. And I did find that as a sweeping sort of broad statement, the 'alleged' connection between slave ownership and country houses and that as a Black woman, trying to come to terms with the erasures that are fact. That these are called into question can be really deflating. So, I suppose it's a question of regrounding myself in the histories that are also written by Black people, like that of Ira Aldridge.[9]

Montserrat's dismay that the term 'alleged' can still be used in the wake of a hefty report that includes evidence of slave-derived wealth from numerous properties, shows that her vital work of recovery, both in this exhibition and over her career, is important to working against both invisibility and denial. Aldridge's narrative allows Montserrat to regroup in the wake of this onslaught of denial. Montserrat is keen to see her work in terms of a tradition of Black women artists campaigning against this sense of invisibility and unbelonging. It has been expressed in the work of Black British women artists like Pollard, Lubaina Himid, Maud Sulter, Claudette Johnson, and Sonia Boyce from the 1980s-90s to the present. It is fitting that a key work in the *Future Collect* exhibition, rescued from obscurity in the public collection of Manchester Art Gallery, is a wonderful self-portrait of the artist's nude torso by Claudette Johnson. Montserrat's own exploration of the vulnerability of her Black body gives this earlier work from a foremother new power, showing a tradition that Montserrat calls upon and develops. This work's troubled history of erasure and amnesia is an exemplar for a process that Johnson herself described, and which is still relevant for Black women artists today:

> The experience of near annihilation is the ghost that haunts the lives of [Black] women in Britain daily. The price of our survival has been the loss of a sense of ownership of both land and body.

[7] Pollard, I. *Postcards Home*, Autograph, 2004, pp. 20-21.
[8] Fowler, C. et al. (eds.) *Interim Report on the Connections between Colonialims and Properties now in the Care of the National Trust Including Links with Historic Slavery*, The National Trust, 2020.
[9] Montserrat, J. *Future Collect Study Day: Jade Montserrat in Conversation with Alan Rice, iniva, 27 May 2021.*

> The ownership of our ancestors' bodies was in the hands of the slave owners. The horrors of slavery and racism have left us with the knowledge that every aspect of our existence is open to abuse...This is reinforced by the experience of a kind of social and cultural invisibility.[10]

Johnson's powerful statement delineates an historical legacy that Montserrat engages with through her work in *Future Collect*, particularly in a series of watercolours, which form a powerful body of work that articulates this invisiblised history. It is not that Black people were never there, it is more that their presence was never acknowledged or witnessed. This elision of Black people in the landscape has led some theorists to describe African diasporic historical presence as 'spectral'. Ian Baucom theorises this absence thus:

> If the general task of what I am calling the testamentary, melancholy realist counterdiscourse of modernity is to recover the lost, to acknowledge and take some affective property in the ruinous 'past', continuously, if non-synchronously, present within now-being, then the particular task of a interested cosmopolitanism...is not merely to make the past present but to render the unseen visible, to bear witness to the truth of what has not been (and cannot have been) witnessed.[11]

Montserrat is engaged with this important work of bearing witness to histories that require part-imagining, or reimagining, because they have been marginalised and invisibilised by the workings of state and colonial power. Montserrat's recovery of the lost history of Black presence renders this unseen population visible, despite their elision from most historical narratives. She literally 'makes the past present' by reinserting the Black body in the frame. She is interested in upturning this legacy, of the elision of past Black histories in these northern environs, and the consequent amnesia that creates a vacuum where Black people once lived, walked and laboured. She wants to give flesh to what have hitherto been ghostly, spectral voices and images. For instance, her 2017 work *You'll have to be on your toes to survive these parts* shows a Black person's feet amidst the British landscape, with a bucolic, red-flowered backdrop. These feet have embedded in them sculptured figures from a different culture, showing that foreign concepts are brought to these lands and enable Black survival in them. Fugitivity is key to this work, showing that Black flight and adaptability have been critical to the survival of cultural integrity. Black agency, despite the overwhelming power of slavery and colonialism is celebrated here and can be linked to hitherto-hidden histories of fugitivity that are only now being brought to the surface.

As evidence for such fugitivity, the runaway advert for a Lancashire slave/servant from the 10 September 1765 edition of the London newspaper, *St. James's Chronicle or the British Evening Post:*

> RUN away from the House of the Rev—Mr. Clarkson, Rector of Heysham, near Lancaster, early in the Morning of Monday the 26th of August last, a Negro Boy, of the Ebo Country, slender made, about five Feet three Inches high, his Left Knee bending inwards, which makes him ha[l]t, a small Lump on his Forehead, with his

[10] Johnson, C. 'Issues Surrounding the Representation of the Naked Body of a Woman', *Feminist Art News*, vol. 3, no. 8, n.d., pp. 12-14, quoted in Eddie Chambers, *Black Artists in British Art History Since the 1950s*, I.B. Tauris, 2014, pp. 145-146.
[11] Baucom, I. *Specters of the Atlantic: Finance Capital, Slavery and the Philosophy of History*, Duke University Press, 2005, p. 218.

Country Marks on his Temples; had on, when eloped, a blue Jacket, a grey Waistcoat, and Leather Breeches; he speaks broad Lancashire Dialect.

Whoever brings him to his Master at Heysham, or to his Master's Brother, Mr. William Clarkson, Surgeon, in Drury-Lane, Leverpoole, shall be handsomely rewarded, and all Charges paid; but whoever harbours him shall be prosecuted with the utmost Rigour of the Law.[12]

Rooted by his Lancashire brogue, the boy routes himself to new, enfranchised worlds congruent with his free African heritage. This is the first written example of a Black man speaking with a Lancashire dialect, a landmark historical discovery. This example is mined by Montserrat, whose praxis of rootedness and routedness mirrors that of such historical exemplars. This connection is always contingent on diasporic movement and this routedness is best approached through Édouard Glissant's notion of 'global errancy' which 'leads from periphery to periphery, makes every periphery into a centre...abolishes the very notion of centre and periphery'.[13] Glissant describes the construction of these multiple histories as key to the making of a new radical historiography 'not saturated with a single history but effervescent with intermingled histories, spread around, rushing to fuse without destroying or reducing each other'.[14]

It is these multiple, interweaved histories of Manchester that Montserrat invokes through *Future Collect*: the intersectional exploitation of Black slave labour in the American South and the grim factory conditions of working-class Lancastrians in the cotton mills. This is true to a commonality of experience which suffuses the archival record, despite its often-meagre offerings in telling working-class and enslaved histories. For instance, in the testimony of ten-year-old Ellen Hootoon before His Majesty's Factory Inquiry Commission in 1833, she told of her brutal treatment at Eccles' Spinning Mill where on one occasion, because she was late, her overseer hung an iron weight of over sixteen pounds on her neck 'and made her walk up and down the factory floor...she fell down several times'.[15] The use of iron restraints and chains, though much more common in slavery, is seen here to occur in factory discipline too. Of course, some experiences are specific to the exploitation of the slave system, and others to the factory system, but many of them speak to experiences of hunger, violence, restraint, and child labour, making the point that the cotton economy was and continues to be a global exploiter of both wage and chattel slaves.

Montserrat's *You'll have to be on your toes to survive these parts* speaks to the legacy of these multiple histories, but specifically to Black agency in a context of exploitation and denial of movement. Literally and figuratively, fugitivity is summoned here as the mode that Black people adopt to survive; nimble mobility and improvisatory gestures are modes that are essential to making a way through an alien landscape that you must continually try and make your home. The way to do this, she shows, is to carry within you your ancestry, the African worldview encapsulated in art objects that render homespace wherever you are. Glissant's theorising of the legacies of enslavement illustrate why naked bodies are so important to Montserrat's renderings in her films, performances, and watercolours. They describe the special status of enslavement that conjures severe displacement, mental and physical, and an attendant nakedness that is visceral:

[12] 'St. James's Chronicle', 10 September 1765. *Runaway Slaves in Britain: Bondage, Freedom and Race in the Eighteenth Century*. (online database)
[13] Glissant, É. *Poetics of Relation*. Wing, Bestsy (trans.) University of Michigan Press, 1997, p. 29.
[14] Glissant, É. *Caribbean Discourse: Selected Essays*. Dash, M.J. (trans.), University of Virginia Press, 1989, p. 154.
[15] Beckert, S. *Empire of Cotton: A Global History*, Vintage, 2014, p. 177.

> The enslaved African is the 'stripped migrant'. He could not bring his tools, the images of his gods, his daily implements, nor could he send news to his neighbours, or hope to bring his family over, or reconstitute his former family in the place of deportation. Naturally the ancestral spirit had not left him, he had not lost the meaning of a former experience. But he will have to fight for centuries in order to recognise its legitimacy.[16]

Montserrat shows how her figure is naked of everything but her ancestral spirit, through the wonderful marking of her past in her fugitive feet. This dynamic rendition of fugitive culture aligns with historical and contemporary forgings of identities on the move. Montserrat talked about the bodily nature of carrying this history at the *Future Collect* Study Day in answer to a question about the vulnerability of being Black in rural northern England:

> An idea of fugitivity and belonging is very real for a lot of people here. And, I would say, the unsafe feeling that you're talking about in reference to my upbringing is one that's shared. And I think that it also is compounded by muscle memory. I believe that there is sort of muscle memory, not just the muscle memory that we accumulate over our lifetimes, whereby this feeling, this unsafe feeling in an environment in which you are alien and you're quite clearly, whether or not you're ingratiating yourself and integrating and embedding yourself, you're still always an outsider. There's that memory. But I do believe that our imperial colonial histories relating to the transatlantic slave trade, I think as those histories surface in each one of our lives. And I would also suggest that, unless you live in a family or you go to a particular school that puts that on the curriculum or that speaks through these histories in your family, that these are huge, shocking understandings to have. And I believe that they surface a muscle memory that creates these traumatic memories...[17]

Montserrat's discussion of a muscle memory here, linking to her status as alien outsider in an alien environment and to traumatic histories is key to her praxis that seeks to embody the past rather than just narrate it. It seeks to bring forth narratives and images from hitherto-forgotten lives abandoned in the archives. From the registers of the Priory Church, Lancaster, one of the few Black women recorded in Lancashire in the eighteenth century: 'Molly, an adult negroe, Nov. 6 1764 (burial recorded Dec. 1 in the same year.)'[18] Jade Montserrat's work begins the articulation of such northern lives, flickering muscle memories for future generations.

[16] Glissant, É. *Caribbean Discourse*, University of Virginia Press, 1991, p. 50.
[17] Montserrat, J. *Future Collect Study Day: Jade Montserrat in Conversation with Alan Rice*, iniva, 27 May 2021.
[18] Anon. *Handlist 69: Sources for Black and Asian History*, Lancashire Records Office, 2007, p.7.

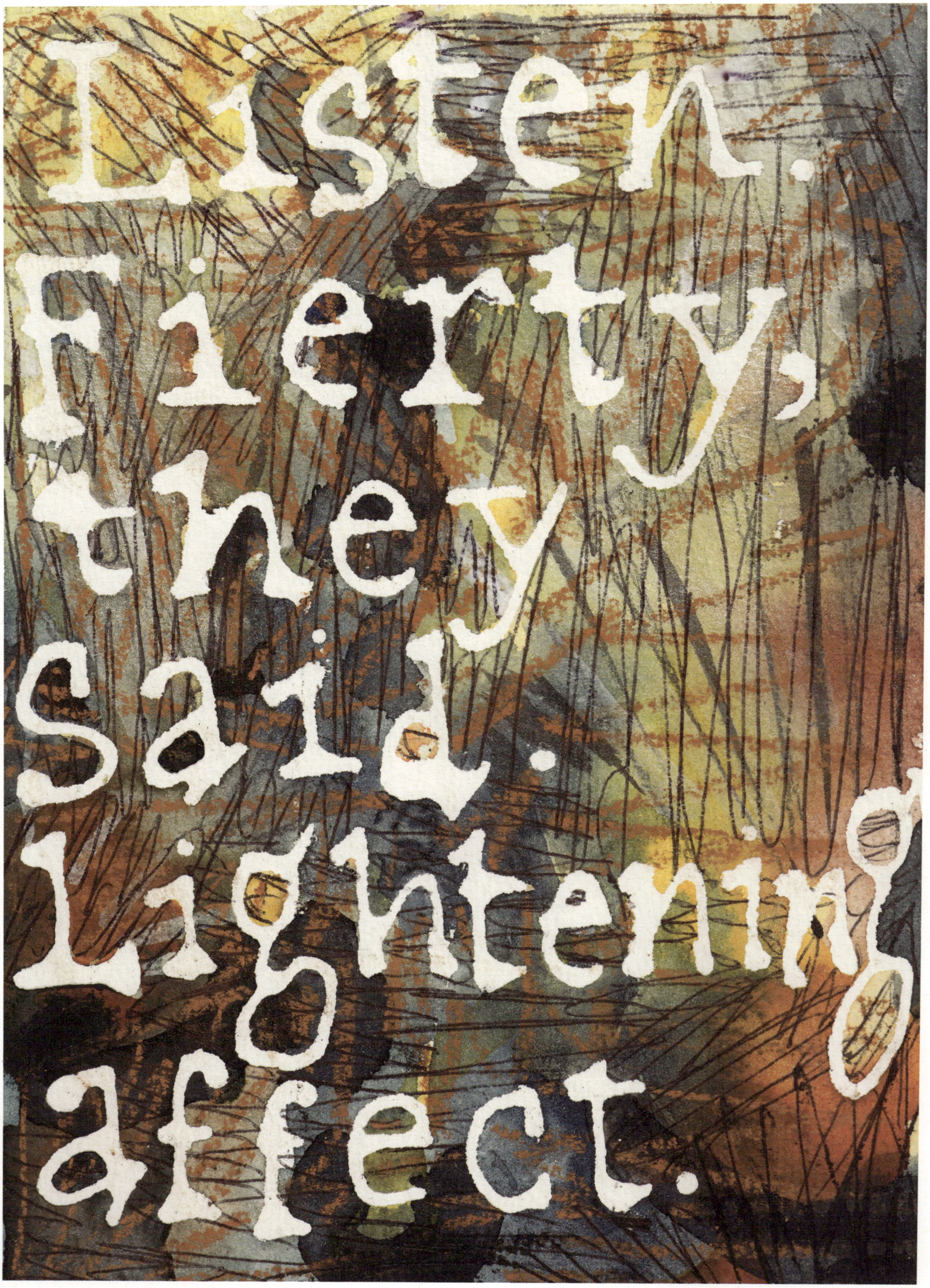

Listen. Fierty, they said. Lightening affect, 2021

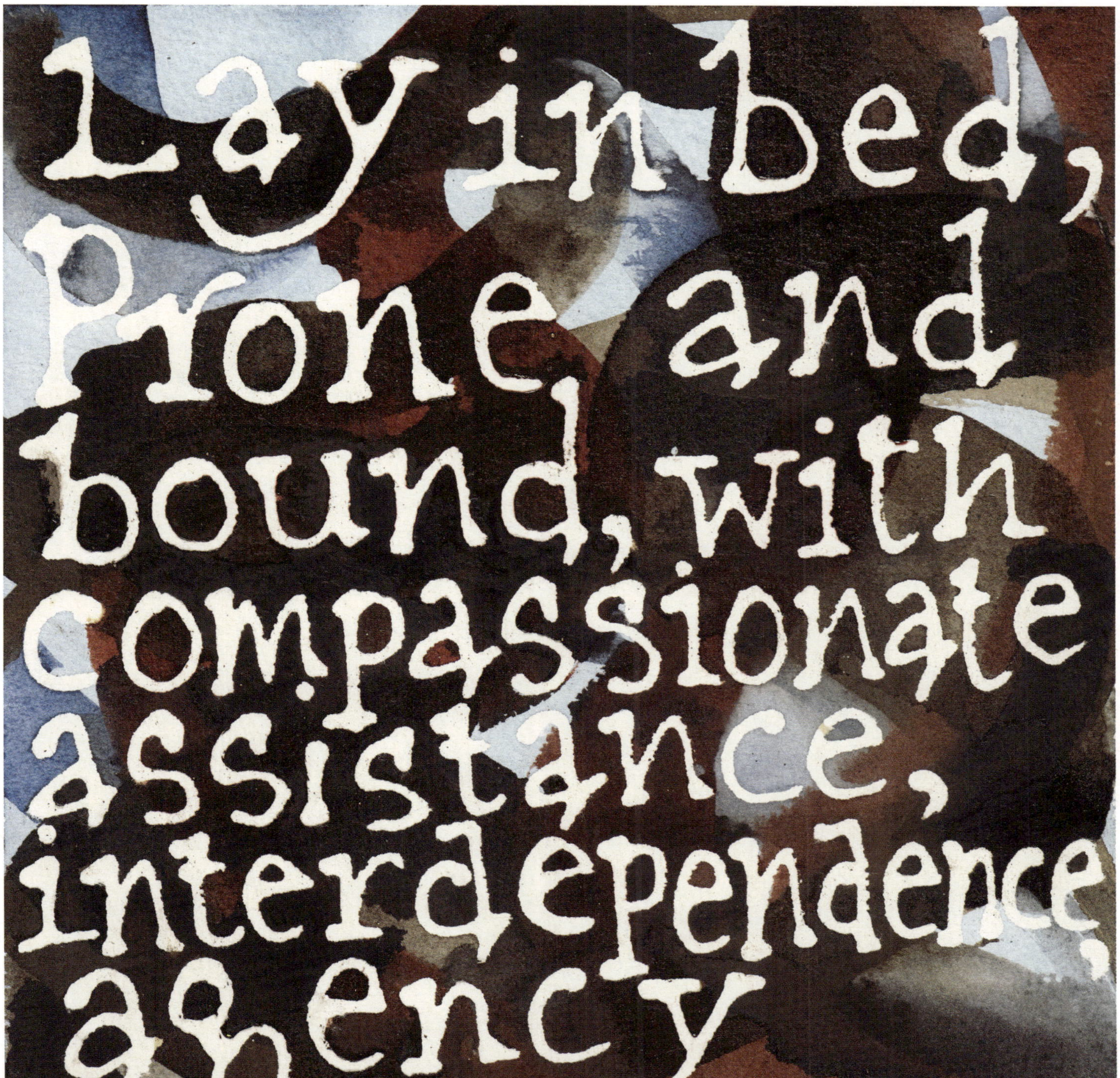

Lay in bed, prone and bound, with compassionate assistance, interdependence, agency, 2021

LIST OF WORKS

LIST OF WORKS BY JADE MONTSERRAT:

Cover: Detail of *I began to distinguish the gleam*, 2017-2020, watercolour, gouache, pencil, pencil crayon, on paper, 46.1 x 36.6cm.

p.2: *To pass the caring on*, 2021, watercolour and ink on card, 14.5 x 29.5cm (image size 14.5 x 15cm)

p.6: *Collected, collective, communal, cultural object through ritual*, 2021, watercolour, ink and pencil crayon on paper, 21 x 14.6cm.

p.20: *Star names shuffled into their corners*, 2021, watercolour on paper, 21 x 14.7cm.

p.21: *The word is prowess, the world and welcome*, 2021, watercolour on paper, 20 x 20cm.

p.45: *Scoring a clean break – cut lines lives cut*, 2021, watercolour, ink and pencil crayon on paper, 21 x 14.8cm.

p.46: *Her body has also responded*, 2021, watercolour, gouache, wax crayon, pencil, ink and oil stick on paper, 21 x 14.7cm.

p.52: *During which I stay home almost all of the time*, 2021, watercolour, gouache and pencil crayon on paper, 10.5 x 14.7cm.

p.80: *You'll have to be on your toes to survive these parts*, 2017, watercolour and pencil crayon on paper, 25 x 17.7cm.

p.88: *Listen. Fierty, they said. Lightening affect*, 2021, watercolour, ink, biro and conte pencil on paper, 21 x 14.7cm.

p.89: *Lay in bed, prone and bound, with compassionate assistance, interdependence, agency*, 2021, watercolour and ink on paper, 20 x 20cm.

p.92: *As a human being*, 2021, watercolour, pencil and felt-tip pen on card, 14.5 x 29.5cm (image size 14.5 x 15cm).

p.93: *What is allowed to be said*, 2021, watercolour and pen on card, 14.5 x 29.5cm (image size 14.5 x 15cm).

p.94: *Head of a negro in his notebook*, 2021, watercolour, graphite and pencil crayon on khadi paper, 15.3 x 11cm.

p.100: *Visual edit of I began to distinguish the gleam*, 2021.

Rehearsal Methods: audition pieces for solo and collective, performance, 2021.

ACKNOWLEDGEMENTS

The *Future Collect* commission has been made possible with thanks, admiration, respect and warmth to an expanded team of artists, thinkers, curators, historians, poets and organisations, listed below.

ACT I
Chloe Austin
Maurice Carlin
Rivca Rubin
Root-ed Zine: Amber Akaunu
Root-ed Zine: Fauziya Johnson

ACT II
Amy Lawrence
Jack Ky Tan

ACT III
Hamja Ahsan
No Matter: Hilary White
No Matter: Jazz Linklater
No Matter: Nell Osborne

Sumuyya Khader: graphic design of Acts I, II and III

COLLECTING PERFORMANCE STUDY DAY
Rose LeJeune
Paul Maheke
Louise O'Kelly
SERAFINE1369
Jon Sharples

REHEARSAL METHODS: AUDITION PIECES FOR SOLO AND COLLECTIVE
Performers: Adelaide Damoah, Nikita Gill, Natasha Howes, Alistair Hudson, Beth Hughes, Dipesh Pandya and Joyce Treasure

IRA ALDRIDGE STUDY DAY
Sandy Nairne
Alan Rice and the Institute for Black Atlantic Research

COLLABORATORS
Bethlem Gallery
Block Universe
Hypertext — Bound Art Book Fair

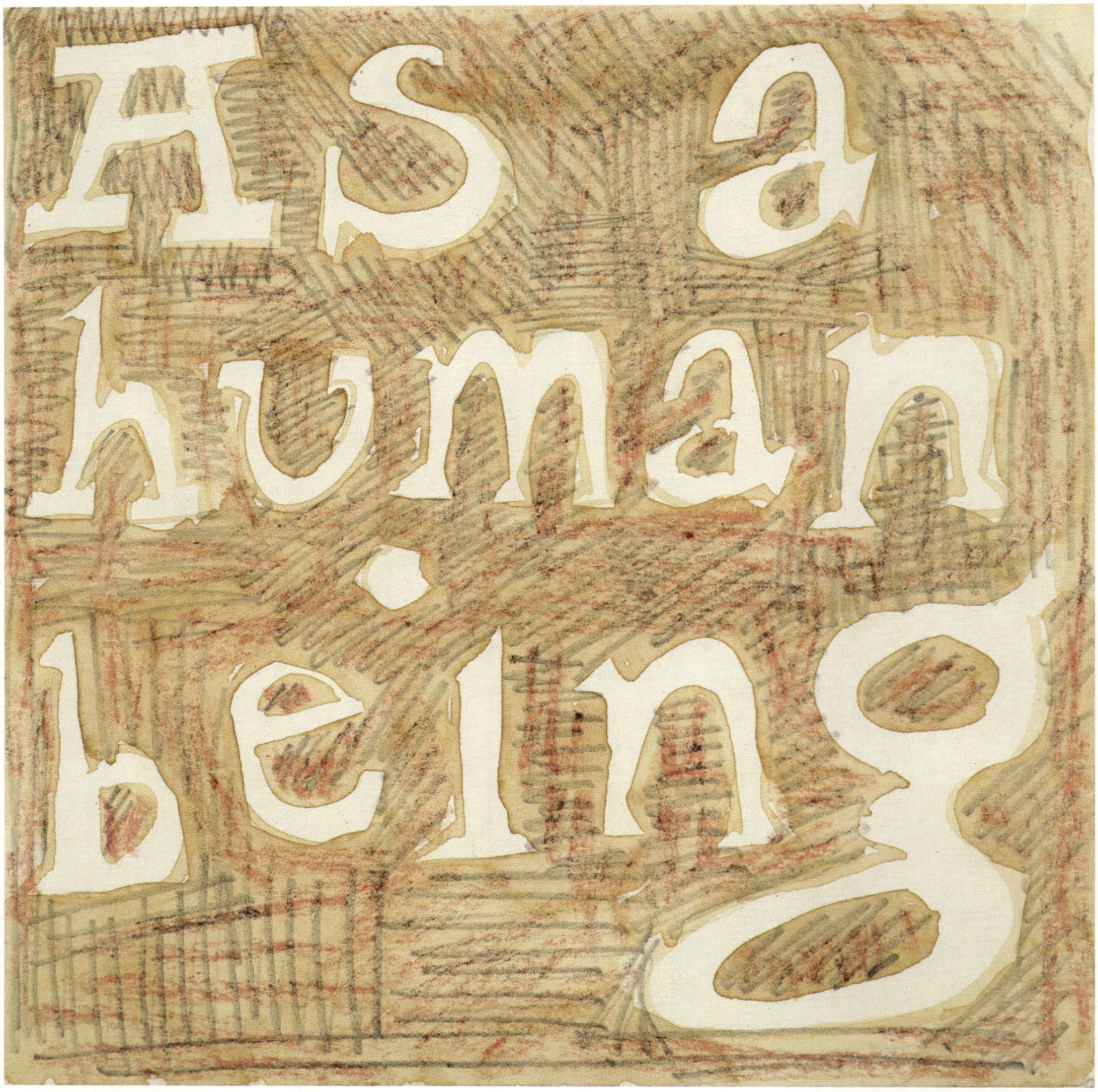

As a human being, 2021

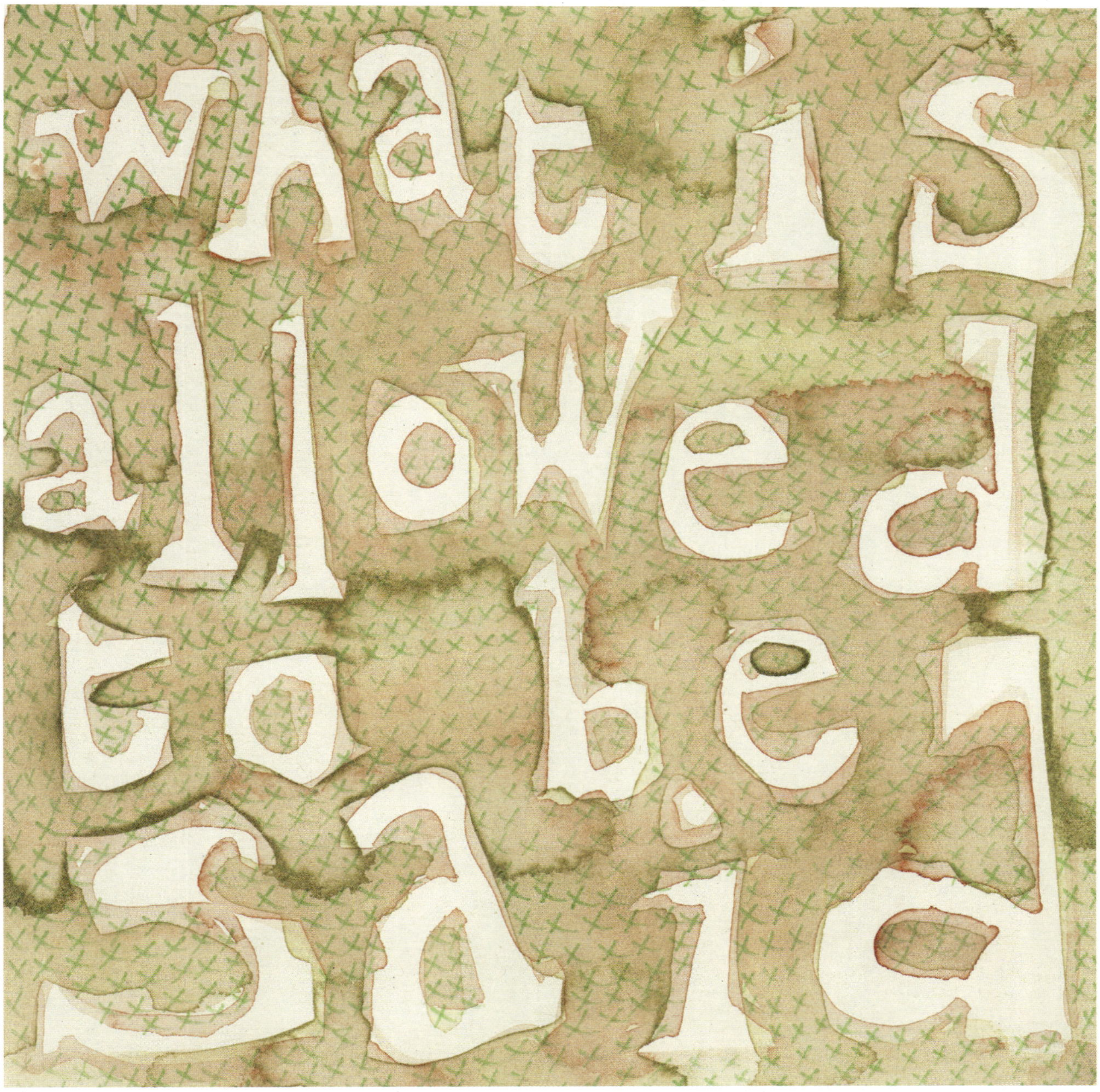

What is allowed to be said, 2021

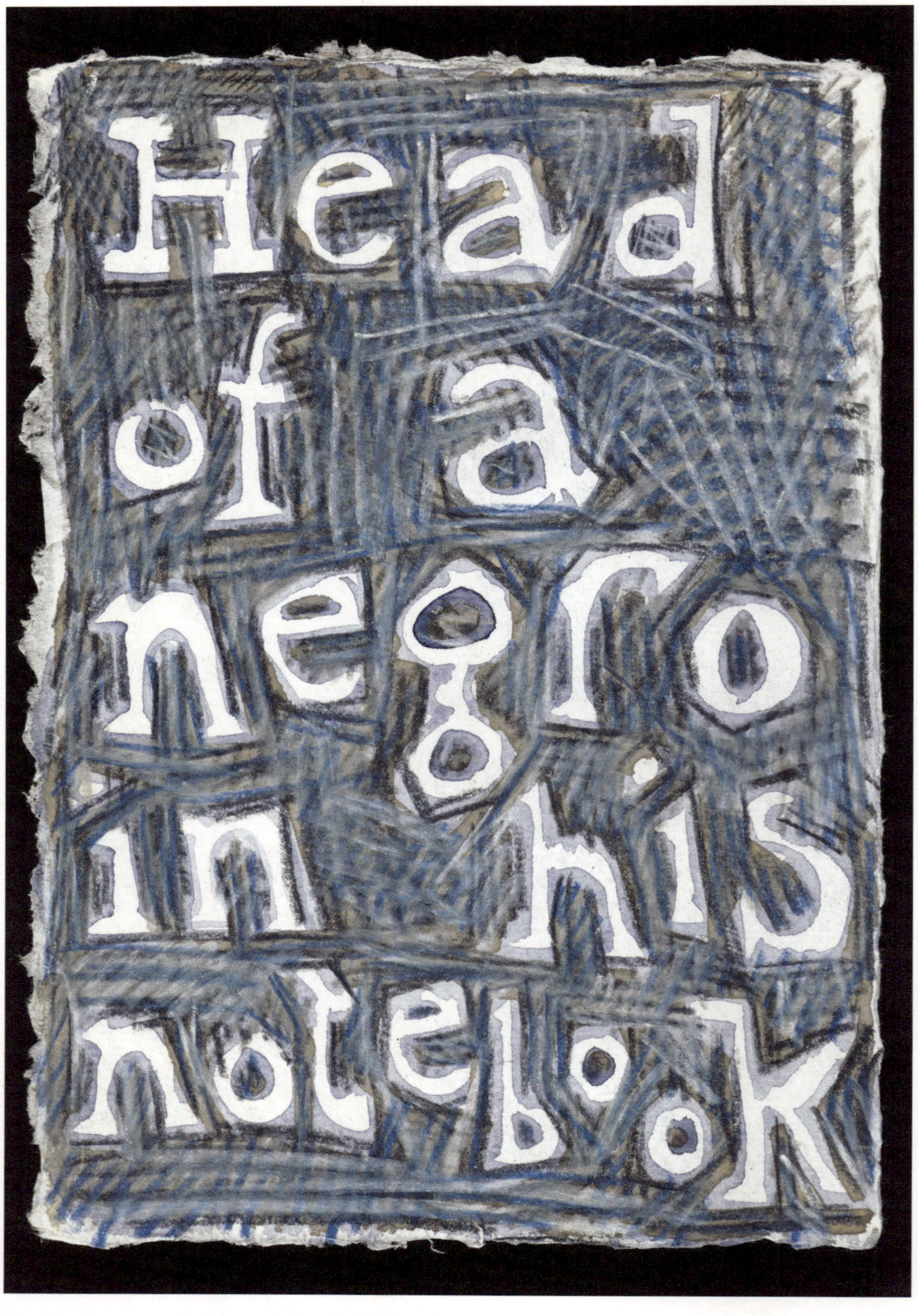

Head of a negro in his notebook, 2021

CONTRIBUTORS

JADE MONTSERRAT'S research-led practice excavates shared histories, alongside delving into her personal narrative. Jade interrogates multiple mediums with the aim to expose gaps in our visual and linguistic habits. She was the recipient of the Stuart Hall Foundation Scholarship, supporting her PhD (via MPhil) at the Institute for Black Atlantic Research at the University of Central Lancaster, (Race and Representation in Northern Britain in the context of the Black Atlantic: A Creative Practice Project) and the development of her work from her Black diasporic perspective in the North of England. She was also awarded one of two Jerwood Student Drawing Prizes in 2017 for *No Need for Clothing*, a documentary photograph of a drawing installation at Cooper Gallery DJCAD by Jacquetta Clark. Jade's *Rainbow Tribe* project — a combination of historical and contemporary manifestations of Black culture from the perspective of the Black diaspora is central to the ways she is producing a body of work, including *No Need for Clothing* and its iterations, as well as her performance work *Revue*. Jade was commissioned to present *Revue* as a 24-hour live performance at SPILL Festival of Performance, October 2018, and a solo exhibition at The Bluecoat, Liverpool in 2019, which toured to Humber Street Gallery in the same year. Montserrat was commissioned by Art on the Underground to create the 2018 Winter Night Tube cover. In 2020, iniva and Manchester Art Gallery have commissioned Jade as the first artist for the project *Future Collect*. As of 2021, Jade is currently in a group exhibition titled *An Infinity of Traces* at Lisson Gallery, and a solo exhibition titled *In Search of Our Mothers' Gardens* at Bosse & Baum Gallery, both in London.

HAMJA AHSAN is an artist, writer, curator and activist currently based in Maastricht, The Netherlands and London, UK. Ahsan's book *Shy Radicals: The Antisystemic Politics of the Militant Introvert*, published in 2017 by Book Works, has been adopted by the neurodiversity movement and was adapted into a film in 2020. In 2019, he adapted the book into *Aspergistan Referendum*, an artwork commissioned for the Ljubljana Biennial of Graphic Arts, where it received the Grand Prize. He was shortlisted for the Liberty Human Rights Award for organising the Free Talha Ahsan campaign, and founded the DIY Cultures Festival of zines and creative activism 2013-17.

AMBER AKAUNU is a Nigerian-German filmmaker, artist and BAFTA scholar from Liverpool. Her work explores themes of belonging, identity, and Black culture. Amber's creative practice also expands to her role as the co-founder and editor of Liverpool-based magazine, *ROOT-ed*. The platform aims to represent the underrepresented and has worked with numerous art institutions and individuals to do just that. In 2020, Amber's first short film, *Afro Hair Rituals*, made its TV debut on BBC 4. The film explores the idea that afro hair is sacred, and the process of styling it can be likened to a ritual, as it is an act that has survived many generations. Amber graduated from university in 2018 with a first-class degree in Fine Art and is now an MA student at Goldsmiths in London, where she studies Screen Documentary.

MAURICE CARLIN is an artist and artistic co-director of Islington Mill. Maurice explores structures and processes within independent peer-led education and is co-founder of Islington Mill Art Academy.

NIKITA GILL is an Afro-Caribbean curator, she was a curator-in-training with iniva and Manchester Art Gallery and is currently Assistant Curator at Manchester Art Gallery. Nikita is interested in unpacking the complicated biographies of objects and acknowledging the voices of those who have been othered within institutions. Her previous work includes support of the exhibition and development of *Excavating the Reno* (2017), *Portraits of Recovery* (2017), *Bodies of Colour* (2018) and *Joy Forever* (2019) at the Whitworth Art Gallery. She has developed and supported performances for Block Universe (2020) Jade Montserrat (2021), Liverpool Biennial and Glasgow International (2021). She is part of *Future Collect*, supporting artist Jade Montserrat's commission. She is also a member of the Black Curators Collective.

INDUSTRIA is an artist-run network, forming working groups to scrutinise institutions and infrastructures in order to imagine and build towards new social universes. Industria is administrated by two artists, who have maintained this shared practice alongside their own artwork and day jobs since 2017. Operating anonymously to avoid taking ownership of work which is collaborative and aims to build coalitions, rather than individual platforms. Industria contextualise themselves for transparency as two, white, cis, and non-disabled women artists in their late twenties living in London, from lower middle and working-class backgrounds. The work Industria does falls across advocacy work in solidarity with artists and cultural workers and produces publications which examine these issues in print.

KATE JESSON is Curator: Modern and Contemporary Art at Manchester Art Gallery. She uses the public collection as a resource to ask questions of identity and Britishness. Past collection displays include *Between the Wars* (2013), *Absent Presence* (2015), *House Proud* (2015), *Goodbye to All That* (2016) and *To Be Human* (2016). Her contemporary exhibitions include solo presentations by Haroon Mirza (2012), Ryan Gander (2014), and Pat Flynn (2015). Kate co-curated the exhibition *Speech Acts* (2018-2019) with Hammad Nasar as an outcome of Black Artists and Modernism (2016-2018). Tania Bruguera's *School of Integration* was co-curated with Shanaz Guzar as part of the Manchester International Festival 2019 and is ongoing. 2020 saw the co-curation of a new *What is Manchester Art Gallery?* introductory display exploring the purpose of our public collections today. It also marked the start of a new partnership with iniva to reimagine the future of collecting.

FAUZIYA JOHNSON is co-founder of *ROOT-ed* zine and an artist working with the medium of photography and drawing. Fuaziya's practice challenges the continual issues of systemic racist practice relating this to the discourse of people's cultural opinions within the Afro-Caribbean community in the UK today.

AMY LAWRENCE is a multimedia artist and producer based in Glasgow (via Manchester), creating fragmented social commentary via performative and visual projects. Lawrence uses choreography and visual arts often in the form of part docu-video, visual and digital projects, performance/liveness and gatherings in arts venues and outside in public spaces. Montage and messiness in series and interrelated projects see solo and collaborative works with ensembles of people and bodies to navigate lived experiences of identity in layering, glitches, personal experiences and reimagining scoring to re-present Black and mixed heritage cultural identities as they exist within the mechanisms of culture and the performance of identity. Amy is Associate Producer at Tramway and Take Me Somewhere Festival, and works as a freelance consultant within arts sector anti-racism and social justice development.

SANDY NAIRNE is a writer and curator based in London, and until 2015 was Director of the National Portrait Gallery in London. He has previously worked at the Institute of Contemporary Arts, London; Arts Council England and as one of two deputy directors at Tate, London. His publications include *State of the Art* (1987) the anthology *Thinking About Exhibitions* (1996), and more recently *The 21st Century Portrait* (2014), *Art Theft and the Case of the Stolen Turners* (2011) and *The Coincidence of Novembers* (2020). He is currently Chair of the Fabric Advisory Committee at St Paul's Cathedral and the Maggie's Art Group for Maggie's Cancer Care Centres. He is a Trustee of the Courtauld Collection, and the National Trust, and a member of the Bank of England Banknote Character Advisory Committee.

NO MATTER is a poetry collective based in Manchester, made up of Jazz Linklater, Nell Osborne and Hilary White. They run a feminist poetry and performance reading series for poetic and performative experiments, and publish work through No Matter Press. In 2019 they were awarded Arts Council England funding for *New Matter*, a series of events with specially commissioned performances from poets and artists.

ROSE NORDIN is a designer and artist in residence at Somerset House studios. She is a founding member of OOMK (One of my Kind) art publishing collective, focused on supporting self-publishing as 'a vehicle to an independent validation to ones' own culture, history, politics and sense of self' (John La Rose). Collectively, OOMK runs community risograph press Rabbits Road Press. Rose functions independently as an artist and graphic designer, with an emphasis on publishing as social practice. She produces publications, visual identities and printed matter, often embedded in educational projects, research residencies or exhibitions. Rose has a focused interest in typography, books as sites of collaboration and the book as an object of representation.

ALAN RICE is Professor in English and American Studies at the University of Central Lancashire (UCLan), Preston, co-director of the Institute for Black Atlantic Research and director of the UCLan Research Centre in Migration, Diaspora and Exile. He has worked on the interdisciplinary study of the Black Atlantic publishing *Radical Narratives of the Black Atlantic* (2003) and *Creating Memorials, Building Identities: The Politics of Memory in the Black Atlantic* (2010). He was a founder member of the Slave Trade Arts Memorial Project in Lancaster which was responsible for unveiling a memorial for victims of the slave trade in 2005 and co-curated *Trade and Empire: Remembering Slavery* at the Whitworth Gallery Manchester in 2007. His latest co-written work is *Inside the Invisible: Memorialising Slavery and Freedom in the Life and Works of Lubaina Himid* (2019). In 2020-21 he is curating the exhibition *Lubaina Himid: Memorial to Zong* for the Lancaster Maritime Museum.

RIVCA RUBIN is a co-director of Islington Mill, a co-instigator of the curatorial team Grand ReUnion, and founder of Upwording, developed with Charles Lauder, a practice of evolutionising thinking through everyday use of language with the aim of creating more harmonious relationships. Upwording seeks to engender a fundamental shift in vocabulary and concepts that are demotivating, hindering and harmful; raising awareness of habitual verbal manifestations of coercion and superiority, terminology that instil and enforce obedience, even within communication that sets out to be helpful. Charles and Rivca also deliver 'Crucial Critical Conversations' a structured programme on how to plan, prepare for and engage in conversations, often thought of as challenging or difficult, with confidence.

JACK KY TAN makes work that explores the connection between the social, the legal and art. Using law, social relations and cultural norms as material, he creates performances, performatives, sculpture, video and participatory projects that highlight the rules — customs, rituals, habits and theories — that guide human behaviour. As part of Tan's social practice, he blurs the boundaries between art, governance and consultancy in order to help organisations reform and re-vision themselves using artistic thinking. Prior to becoming an artist, Tan trained as a lawyer and worked in civil litigation as well as in NGOs undertaking human rights cases, policy and anti-racist campaigning work. He then studied ceramics, obtaining a BA from the University of Westminster and an MA from the Royal College of Art. Tan completed his PhD in legal aesthetics and performance at the University of Roehampton, Dept of Drama, Theatre and Performance.

IMAGE CREDITS

ALL WORKS, UNLESS OTHERWISE STATED, ARE BY JADE MONTSERRAT © THE ARTIST.

p.4: *Ira Aldridge in the Role of Shakespeare's Othello*, c.1826, William Mulready, oil on panel, 40.54 x 29.9 cm. Courtesy of The Walters Art Museum, Baltimore.

p.10: *Ira Aldridge as Othello, the Moor of Venice*, 1826, James Northcote, oil on canvas, 76.2 x 63.5 cm. Courtesy of Manchester Art Gallery,
Photo: Michael Pollard.

Previously titled *Head of a Negro in the Character of Othello* (1826), *Othello, the Moor of Venice* (1827) and *A Moor* (1846). Title changed to *Ira Aldridge as Othello, the Moor of Venice* in 2020.

p.19: ©Sonia Boyce. All Rights Reserved, DACS 2021. Image courtesy of Manchester Art Gallery,
Photo: Andrew Brooks.

p.22: *Head of a Man (?Ira Frederick Aldridge)*, exhibited 1827, John Simpson, oil on canvas, 73.3 × 56.2 cm. Tate; Photo: Tate.

p.30: *Ira Aldridge as Othello*, c.1830, Henry Perronet Briggs, oil on canvas, 128.3 x 103.5 cm. Courtesy of National Portrait Gallery, Smithsonian Institution.

p.38: Courtesy of the Artist, © Jack Ky Tan.

p.40: Getty Research Institute, Los Angeles (2006.M.24).

p.54-59: Courtesy of the Artist and Manchester Art Gallery. Photos: Michael Pollard.

p.60-63: Courtesy of the Artist and Manchester Art Gallery.

p.64: Courtesy of the Artist and Manchester Art Gallery. Photo: Michael Pollard.

p.66: *Ira Aldridge as Othello in 'Othello'* by William Shakespeare, c. 1848, Unknown Artist, oil on canvas, 42.8 x 34.3 cm. © Victoria and Albert Museum, London.

p.76: Courtesy of Live Art Development Agency and Lois Weaver.

p.78: Courtesy Split Britches and Lois Weaver.

p.102: © RSC / Shakespeare Birthplace Trust.

Poster: Courtesy Bobby Sands Trust.

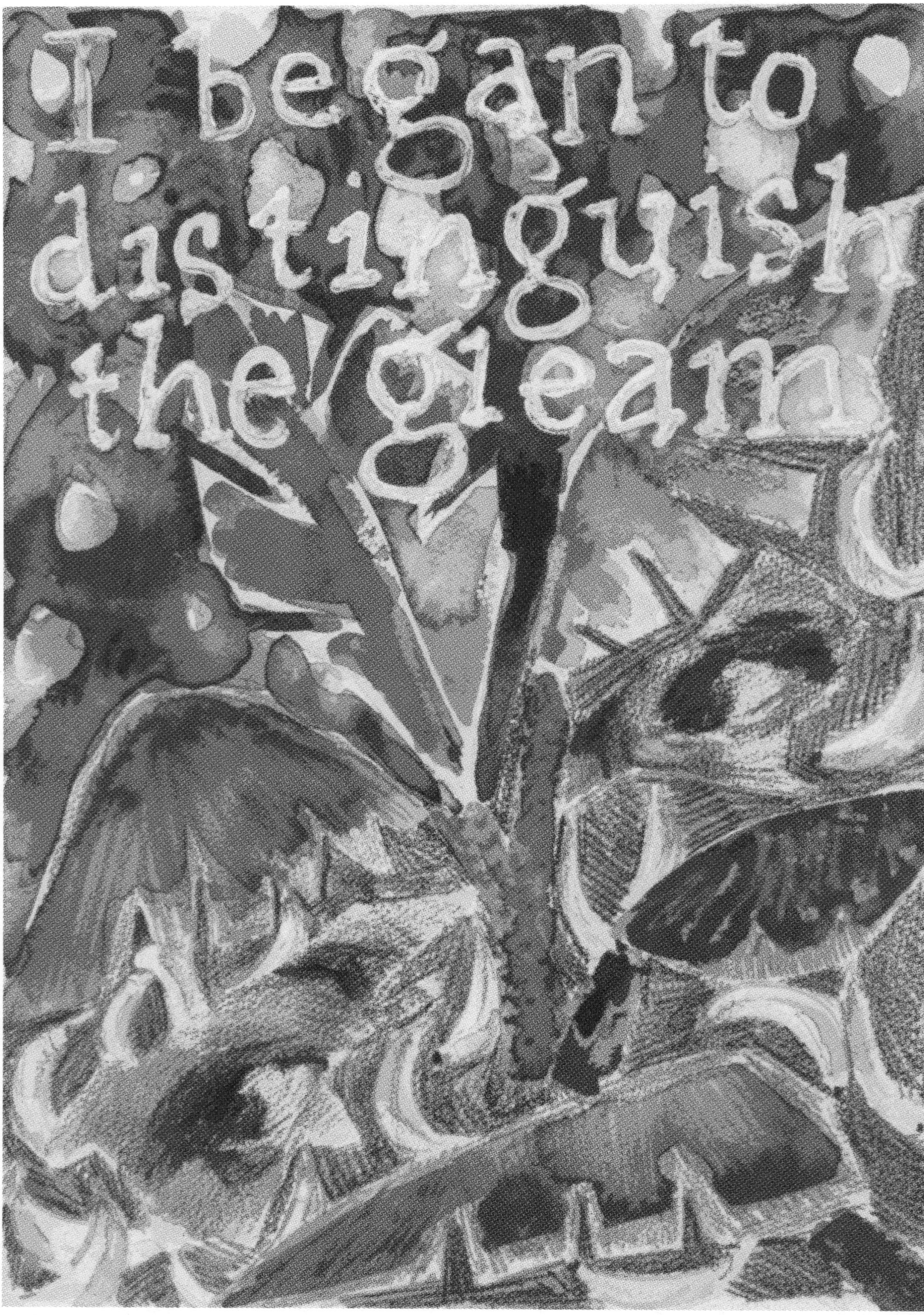

Visual edit of *I began to distinguish the gleam*, 2021

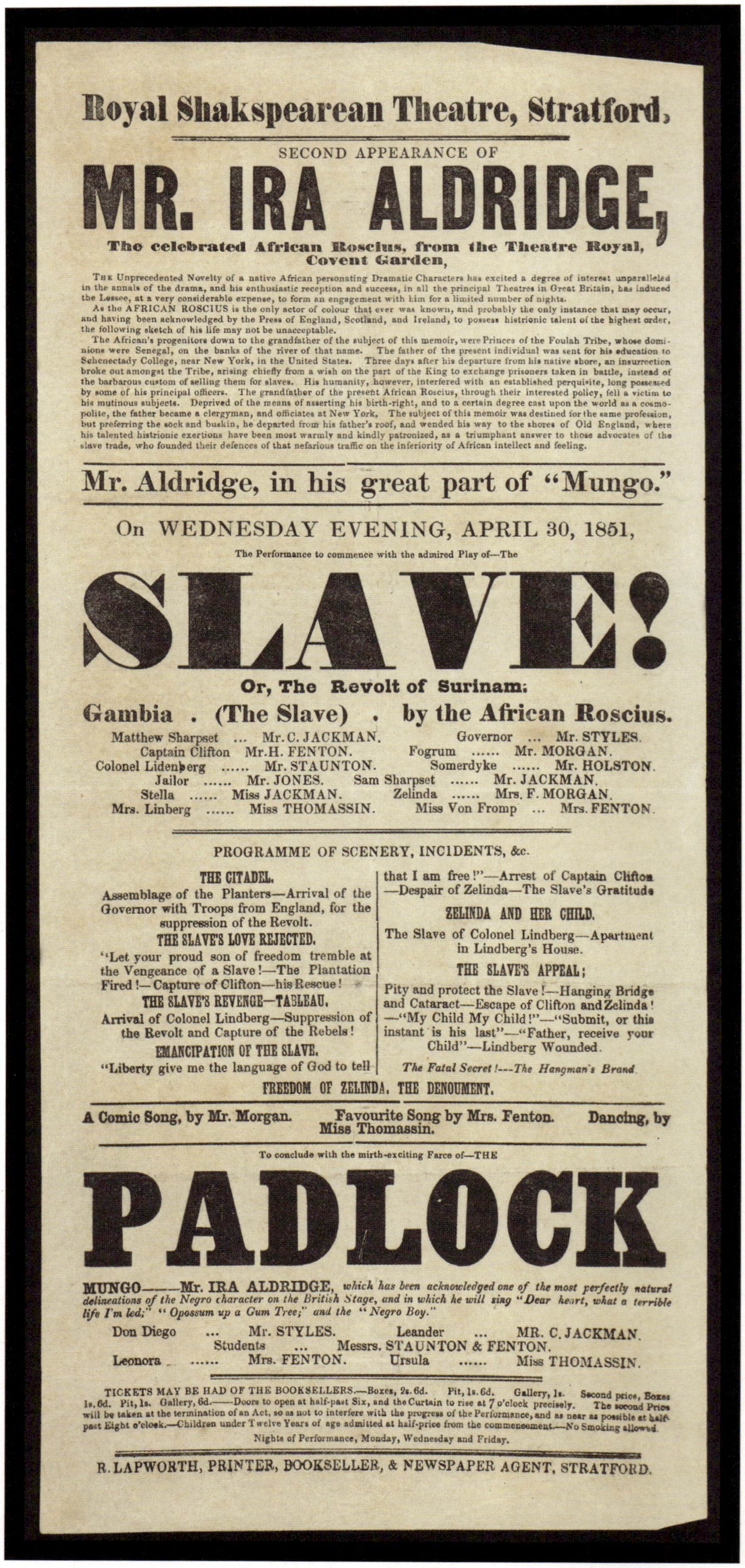

Royal Shakspearean Theatre, Stratford,

SECOND APPEARANCE OF

MR. IRA ALDRIDGE,

The celebrated African Roscius, from the Theatre Royal, Covent Garden,

THE Unprecedented Novelty of a native African personating Dramatic Characters has excited a degree of interest unparalleled in the annals of the drama, and his enthusiastic reception and success, in all the principal Theatres in Great Britain, has induced the Lessee, at a very considerable expense, to form an engagement with him for a limited number of nights.

As the AFRICAN ROSCIUS is the only actor of colour that ever was known, and probably the only instance that may occur, and having been acknowledged by the Press of England, Scotland, and Ireland, to possess histrionic talent of the highest order, the following sketch of his life may not be unacceptable.

The African's progenitors down to the grandfather of the subject of this memoir, were Princes of the Foulah Tribe, whose dominions were Senegal, on the banks of the river of that name. The father of the present individual was sent for his education to Schenectady College, near New York, in the United States. Three days after his departure from his native shore, an insurrection broke out amongst the Tribe, arising chiefly from a wish on the part of the King to exchange prisoners taken in battle, instead of the barbarous custom of selling them for slaves. His humanity, however, interfered with an established perquisite, long possessed by some of his principal officers. The grandfather of the present African Roscius, through their interested policy, fell a victim to his mutinous subjects. Deprived of the means of asserting his birth-right, and to a certain degree cast upon the world as a cosmopolite, the father became a clergyman, and officiates at New York. The subject of this memoir was destined for the same profession, but preferring the sock and buskin, he departed from his father's roof, and wended his way to the shores of Old England, where his talented histrionic exertions have been most warmly and kindly patronized, as a triumphant answer to those advocates of the slave trade, who founded their defences of that nefarious traffic on the inferiority of African intellect and feeling.

Mr. Aldridge, in his great part of "Mungo."

On WEDNESDAY EVENING, APRIL 30, 1851,

The Performance to commence with the admired Play of—The

SLAVE!

Or, The Revolt of Surinam:

Gambia . (The Slave) . by the African Roscius.

Matthew Sharpset ... Mr. C. JACKMAN. Governor ... Mr. STYLES.
Captain Clifton Mr. H. FENTON. Fogrum ...... Mr. MORGAN.
Colonel Lidenberg ...... Mr. STAUNTON. Somerdyke ...... Mr. HOLSTON.
Jailor ...... Mr. JONES. Sam Sharpset ...... Mr. JACKMAN.
Stella ...... Miss JACKMAN. Zelinda ...... Mrs. F. MORGAN.
Mrs. Linberg ...... Miss THOMASSIN. Miss Von Fromp ... Mrs. FENTON.

PROGRAMME OF SCENERY, INCIDENTS, &c.

THE CITADEL.
Assemblage of the Planters—Arrival of the Governor with Troops from England, for the suppression of the Revolt.
THE SLAVE'S LOVE REJECTED.
"Let your proud son of freedom tremble at the Vengeance of a Slave!—The Plantation Fired!—Capture of Clifton—his Rescue!
THE SLAVE'S REVENGE—TABLEAU.
Arrival of Colonel Lindberg—Suppression of the Revolt and Capture of the Rebels!
EMANCIPATION OF THE SLAVE.
"Liberty give me the language of God to tell that I am free!"—Arrest of Captain Clifton—Despair of Zelinda—The Slave's Gratitude
ZELINDA AND HER CHILD.
The Slave of Colonel Lindberg—Apartment in Lindberg's House.
THE SLAVE'S APPEAL;
Pity and protect the Slave!—Hanging Bridge and Cataract—Escape of Clifton and Zelinda!—"My Child My Child!"—"Submit, or this instant is his last"—"Father, receive your Child"—Lindberg Wounded.
The Fatal Secret!---The Hangman's Brand.
FREEDOM OF ZELINDA. THE DENOUMENT.

A Comic Song, by Mr. Morgan. Favourite Song by Mrs. Fenton. Dancing, by Miss Thomassin.

To conclude with the mirth-exciting Farce of—THE

PADLOCK

MUNGO——Mr. IRA ALDRIDGE, *which has been acknowledged one of the most perfectly natural delineations of the Negro character on the British Stage, and in which he will sing "Dear heart, what a terrible life I'm led;" "Opossum up a Gum Tree;" and the "Negro Boy."*

Don Diego ... Mr. STYLES. Leander ... MR. C. JACKMAN.
Students ... Messrs. STAUNTON & FENTON.
Leonora ...... Mrs. FENTON. Ursula ...... Miss THOMASSIN.

TICKETS MAY BE HAD OF THE BOOKSELLERS.—Boxes, 2s. 6d. Pit, 1s. 6d. Gallery, 1s. Second price, Boxes 1s. 6d. Pit, 1s. Gallery, 6d.——Doors to open at half-past Six, and the Curtain to rise at 7 o'clock precisely. The second Price will be taken at the termination of an Act, so as not to interfere with the progress of the Performance, and as near as possible at half-past Eight o'clock.—Children under Twelve Years of age admitted at half-price from the commencement.—No Smoking allowed.

Nights of Performance, Monday, Wednesday and Friday.

R. LAPWORTH, PRINTER, BOOKSELLER, & NEWSPAPER AGENT, STRATFORD.

Playbill — *Slave! and Padlock* at the Royal Shakespearean Theatre, 1951, Stratford

COLOPHON

Published by the Institute of International Visual Arts (iniva) in association with Manchester Art Gallery in September 2021 on the occasion of the opening of Jade Montserrat's *Future Collect* Commission *Constellations: Care & Resistance* at Manchester Art Gallery. This artist publication was initiated and curated by Jade Montserrat, edited by Industria.

A Reimagining of Relations is accompanied by additional printed inserts: a Bibliography (presented in three bookmarks), a poster of a Bobby Sands solidarity protest and the performance score for *Rehearsal Methods: audition pieces for solo and collective*, 2021 by Jade Montserrat.

© 2021 iniva and Jade Montserrat

Institute of International Visual Arts (iniva)
16 John Islip St,
London, SW1P 4JU, UK

Images © 2021, to the credited copyright holders and artists, unless otherwise stated.
Text © 2021, the authors.

Printed in 2021, London, UK.

Managing Editor: Anahí Saravia Herrera
Editors: Industria
Copy Editor: Jay Drinkall
Design and Layout: Rose Nordin
Printing and binding: Kingsbury Press
Paper: Nautilus Classic 120gsm
Typefaces: Tobias (modified to include Eye-ra Aldridge glyph) and Benton Sans
Edition: 1000

Future Collect team:
iniva Artistic Director: Sepake Angiama
iniva Future Collect Project Manager: Rohini Malik Okon
Curator at Manchester Art Gallery: Kate Jesson
Curator-in-training at iniva and Manchester Art Gallery: Nikita Gill
Future Commons Coordinator: Priya Jay
Evaluator: Dr Alison Rooke

ISBN 978-1-899846-62-7
Published by STUART as an imprint of iniva.

A catalogue record of this book is available from the British Library.

All rights reserved. No part of this publication should be reproduced, stored in any retrieval system or transmitted in any form, or by any means, electronic, mechanical or otherwise without prior permission in writing from the publisher and the artist.

Great care has been taken to identify all image copyright holders correctly. In cases of errors or omissions please contact the publisher so that we can make corrections in future editions.

This publication and the *Future Collect* project are supported by Arts Council England, Art Fund and the Esmée Fairbairn Foundation.

Manchester Art Gallery
iniva
STUART
LOTTERY FUNDED
Supported using public funding by ARTS COUNCIL ENGLAND
Esmée Fairbairn FOUNDATION
Art Fund_